ECDL Module 5: Database

Springer
London
Berlin
Heidelberg
New York
Barcelona
Hong Kong
Milan
Paris
Singapore
Tokyo

ECDL Module 5: Database

ECDL – the European PC standard

by **Bill McTaggart**

Springer

BCS

The Publisher and the BCS would like to publicly acknowledge the vital support of the ECDL Foundation in validating and approving this book for the purpose of studying for the European-wide ECDL qualification.

Springer-Verlag London Ltd, Sweetapple House, Catteshall Road, Godalming, Surrey GU7 3DJ or

The British Computer Society, 1 Sanford Street, Swindon, Wiltshire SN1 1HJ

ISBN 1-85233-446-0

British Library Cataloguing in Publication Data
McTaggart, Bill
ECDL module 5: database: ECDL – the European PC standard. – (European computer driving licence)
1. Databases
I. Title
005.7

ISBN 1852334460

Printed and bound at The Cromwell Press, Trowbridge, Wiltshire, England.
34/3830-543210 Printed on acid-free paper SPIN 10792528

Preface

This book is intended to help you successfully complete the test for Module 5 of the European Computer Driving Licence (ECDL). However before we start working through the actual content of the guide you may find it useful to know a little bit more about the ECDL in general and where this particular Module fits into the overall framework.

What Is The ECDL?

The European Computer Driving Licence (ECDL) is a European-wide qualification that enables people to demonstrate their competence in computer skills. It certifies the candidate's knowledge and competence in personal computer usage at a basic level and is based upon a single agreed syllabus.

This syllabus covers a range of specific knowledge areas and skill sets, which are broken down into seven modules. Each of the modules must be passed before the ECDL certificate can be awarded, though they may be taken in any order but must be completed within a three year period.

Testing of candidates is at audited testing centres, and successful completion of the test will demonstrate the holder's basic knowledge and competence in using a personal computer and common computer applications.

The implementation of the ECDL in the UK is being managed by the British Computer Society. It is growing at a tremendous rate and is set to become the most widely recognised qualification in the field of work-related computer use.

The ECDL Modules

The seven modules which make up the ECDL certificate are described briefly below:

Module 1: Basic Concepts of Information Technology covers the physical make-up of a personal computer and some of the basic concepts of Information Technology such as data storage and memory, and the uses of information networks within computing. It also looks at the application of computer software in society and the use of IT systems in everyday situations. Some basic security and legal issues are also addressed.

Module 2: Using the Computer and Managing Files covers the basic functions of a personal computer and its operating system. In particular it looks at operating effectively within the desktop environment, managing and organising files and directories, and working with desktop icons.

Module 3: Word Processing covers the use of a word processing application on a personal computer. It looks at the basic operations associated with creating, formatting and finishing a word processing document ready for distribution. It also addresses some of the more advanced features such as creating standard tables, using pictures and images within a document, importing objects and using mail merge tools.

Module 4: Spreadsheets covers the basic concepts of spreadsheets and the ability to use a spreadsheet application on a personal computer. Included are the basic operations for developing, formatting and using a spreadsheet, together with the use of basic formulas and functions to carry out standard mathematical and logical operations. Importing objects and creating graphs and charts are also covered.

Module 5: Database covers the basic concepts of databases and the ability to use a database on a personal computer. It addresses the design and planning of a simple database, and the retrieval of information from a database through the use of query, select and sort tools.

Module 6: Presentation covers the use of presentation tools on a personal computer, in particular creating, formatting and preparing presentations. The requirement to create a variety of presentations for different audiences and situations is also addressed.

Module 7: Information and Communication is divided into two main sections, the first of which covers basic Web search tasks using a Web browser and search engine tools. The second section addresses the use of electronic mail software to send and receive messages, to attach documents, and to organise and manage message folders and directories.

This guide focuses upon Module 5.

How To Use This Guide

The purpose of this guide is to take you through all of the knowledge areas and skill sets specified in the syllabus for Module 5. The use of clear, non technical explanations and self paced exercises will provide you with an understanding of the key elements of the syllabus and give you a solid foundation for moving on to take the ECDL test relating to this Module. All exercises contained within this guide are based upon the Windows 98 operating system and Office 97 software.

Each chapter has a well defined set of objectives that relate directly to the syllabus for the ECDL Module 5. Because the guide is structured in a logical sequence you are advised to work through the chapters one at a time from the beginning. Throughout each chapter there are various review questions so that you can determine whether you have understood the principles involved correctly prior to moving on to the next step.

Conventions Used In This Guide

Throughout this guide you will come across notes alongside a number of icons. They are all designed to provide you with specific information related to the section of the book you are currently working through. The icons and the particular types of information they relate to are as follows:

information

Additional Information: Further information or explanation about a specific point.

caution!

Caution: A word of warning about the risks associated with a particular action, together with guidance, where necessary on how to avoid any pitfalls.

definition

Definition: A plain English definition of a newly introduced term or concept.

shortcut

Short Cuts: Short cuts and hints for using a particular program more effectively.

As you are working through the various exercises contained within this guide, you will be asked to carry out a variety of actions:

- Where we refer to commands or items that you are required to select from the PC screen, then we indicate these in bold, for example: Click on the **Yes** button.
- Where you are asked to key text in to the PC, then we indicate this in italics, for example: Type in the words '*Saving my work*'.

You should now be in a position to use this guide, so lets get started. Good luck!

Contents

1

Introduction

In this chapter you will learn how to

- *Define and describe data and information.*
- *Explain the need for, and advantages of, databases.*
- *Describe some applications of databases.*
- *Recognise the difference between a database and a database management system.*
- *Describe the basic principles of a relational database management system.*
- *Explain the storage of data in tables.*
- *Define the roles of queries, forms and reports.*

This guide is intended to help you develop your skills in both building and querying databases in order to obtain useful information in the form of reports and other types of output. We do not assume any previous exposure to databases and we will avoid most of the technical background that underpins database systems. By the end of this guide you will have covered all the skill sets and task items defined for the ECDL Module 5 and will be ready to pass the practice-based test.

The best way to learn about a new subject is usually to do something practical. We will adopt this approach throughout the guide, during which we will develop a simple database to store information about a collection of music CDs. We will also use a sample database provided by Microsoft that will show what can be achieved when you have attained a good level of familiarity with Access.

1.1. Using This Guide

The guide is divided into six chapters, five of which cover major components of Access 97. This chapter is the exception and covers some of the basic ideas that are common to all database systems. Each chapter has a well-defined set of objectives that relate directly to the syllabus for the ECDL Module 5. You can gauge your progress by the achievement of these objectives. You should work through the chapters in sequence, because each chapter builds on the last using the CD database as the core of your practical work.

1.2. Data, Databases and Information

First we need to define what we mean when we talk about data and storing it in databases.

We can start with a definition of a database:

d
definition

A database is a collection of related data.

This helps, but still leaves us rather unclear about what is meant by data. We tend to use this word in normal conversation in a very general way, without being too concerned about what it actually means. A further definition will clarify the meaning.

d
definition

Data is known facts about something that can be recorded and stored

To record something means that we have some way of taking a fact and writing it down on paper or turning it into some electrical signals that can be stored in a computer system.

In our definition of database, we talked about related data. This emphasises that our collection of facts is not just a random collection of facts about anything. They must be organised and focussed on a particular topic area. We will keep referring back to this idea of organising data, because it is fundamental to understanding databases. A collection of facts is not particularly useful on its own. It is like a pile of bricks delivered off the back of a lorry. We have to arrange the bricks in some sensible way to get a building. We could actually produce lots of buildings from the same pile of bricks. The same is true of data. We can apply this analogy to see how we use a collection of data.

d
definition

Information is derived from data and is useful in solving problems. Information is the meaning that a person assigns to data by means of the known conventions used in its representation.

This means that data becomes useful information when we put it together to solve a real problem. The facts that we have stored are not really useful in themselves, but they can become information when we apply what we know about the facts to draw conclusions from them. This is a very important idea. Databases store data, but are really only useful when we can extract information from them in a useful way. We will devote three full chapters of this guide to the ways in which we can carry out this extraction process.

1.3. Database Management Systems

We have defined database, but you know already that there are database programs such as Access 97. Are these databases in the way we have defined them? The answer is no; Access 97 is not a collection of related data. Programs such as Access 97 are really database management systems.

definition

A database management system (DBMS) is a collection of programs that enables users to create and maintain a database.

Taking our pile of bricks analogy a little further, we can think of a database management system as the tools that we need to put together a useful building using the bricks.

Another way of thinking about a DBMS is to compare it with a word processor. We use a word processor to put together and maintain a document. The word processor simply gives us the tools needed to type, organise, store and print words. A database management system like Access 97 does exactly the same thing for a collection of data. Database Management Systems have been around for a long time, far longer than PCs have existed. There is more than one type of DBMS, but most recent systems use a similar approach to the way they structure and relate data. They are based on some simple, yet powerful ideas and rules that we know work well for most business applications of databases. The simple idea is that we can store and organise data in tables. Database Management Systems that use these simple table based ideas are called Relational Database Management Systems (RDBMS).

caution!

Many people believe that the word relational comes from the fact that we are storing collections of related data. This is not so. The word relational comes from the underlying theory of this type of database management system that is based on the mathematical word for a table, which is a relation.

Access 97 is a relational database management system and it shares many of its basic ideas with a lot of other database management systems that run on all kinds of computers from PCs up to enormous mainframes. This doesn't mean that you could run Access 97 on such machines!

1.4. Uses of Databases

We have defined a database as a collection of related data, but we recognise that for it to be useful, we must be able to extract information from the database in a variety of different ways. Some databases are used in just this way, as a place to deposit data and return it as information at a later date. A more useful way of employing a database is as the foundation for a more complete computer application; a computer system that is designed to carry out a significant business function.

Typical business applications are:

- A Personnel system keeping records about employees, their grades, training and employment history.
- An Accounts system that keeps data about all the transactions that a company makes. The accounts system will produce a wide variety of reports, and will automate some functions such as the calculation of Value Added Tax.
- A Customer Relations Management system will keep records of all a businesses' current and potential customers. The system will remind sales people when they should follow up a sales lead and record what information has been sent to all the potential customers.

Exercise 1.1

Try to think of an application that is likely to use a database. Hint - these applications usually use a lot of data.

Each of these three applications would normally be built on top of a database. This gives the system designers a lot of help and avoids them having to recreate a lot of standard building blocks. Writing computer programs that work with databases goes beyond the syllabus for this module, but you should be aware that this is very common and that Access 97 provides a rich set of tools for creating an application in this way.

1.5. Relational Databases

We have already stated that most modern database management systems are based on the relational model.

information

Relational model is just a sophisticated way of saying 'based on tables'.

We don't need to understand all the theory that led to the relational model, but we certainly need to understand the basic ideas.

All data in a relational database is organised in tables. Each row in a table contains a single set of facts about a thing that we are interested in. All the rows in a table are laid out in the same way with the same columns. Each column specifies a different part of the fact that we are recording. To illustrate this, consider an employee table that might be part of a personnel database, as shown in Figure 1.1.

First Name	Initials	Last Name	Social Security Number	Grade
John		Williamson	1285TN1	3
Marie	S	Dupont	6589AF7	1
Luigi		Moretti	8762KQ9	3
Henry	N	Porter	5672HF2	2
Wilma	W	Wimble	8712DE4	3

Figure 1.1 An employee table.

Notice that each row represents facts about a different employee. For example, the first row says that we have an employee called John Williamson with a Social Security number of 1285TN1 and a grade of 3. The first column is called First Name and contains the first name of every employee. Every column has a name and all the rows in that column contain the same type of information. For example the Social Security Number contains only social security numbers and nothing else. In a table, we have only one fact at the junction of every row and column. We don't try to cram everything into one or two columns; this is important.

A relational database consists of a series of such tables. Each table stores a set of facts about a separate thing, and every table has a name. This simple idea is powerful enough to enable us to build extremely complex databases. In Chapter 3 we will see how we can decide what tables we need for a database and how we can set up these tables in Access 97.

1.6. Queries, Forms and Reports

Storing data in tables is the basis of the relational model, but we need to be able to get information from those tables to make a database useful. We also need to add to and change the data in the tables. Ideally we would want to see information in a more attractive and familiar form than just plain tables. We can achieve all of these objectives by using Queries, Forms and Reports.

definition

A query extracts the data we want from one or more tables and presents it to us as another table.

You should notice that a query works with tables and produces tables. This is in line with our relational thinking that insists that all data in our database is stored in tables and nothing else.

We can design queries to extract the data we require, then store the query for future use any time we need that data again.

definition

A form is used to enter, change, view and print data in one or more tables or queries.

We can design forms so that they resemble paper forms, or we can make them much more interactive, with pictures and even sounds if we wish. Forms are the human face that your database will present to the people who use your database whilst sitting in front of a screen.

definition

A report is a printed output from a database, suitable for people who need information away from a computer screen.

You can use a lot of imagination in the design of reports. Access provides some good tools for producing really professional looking reports. In a business context, reports are an essential feature of any database management system.

We will cover Queries, Forms and Reports in Chapters 4, 5 and 6 of this guide.

1.7. Some Conventions

This guide uses practical examples very extensively. We will describe the steps that you can take to follow these examples using a few conventions. We will use the following words to represent common Windows features and actions.

- An icon is a small picture, usually representing an action that you want the computer to perform.
- A button is a small rectangular area with a command written it. Sometimes the command will be represented by a picture instead of text. Typical buttons are OK, CANCEL, QUIT etc.
- A window is a rectangular area displayed on the screen. It will have borders and you can usually shift the window around the screen and adjust the positions of the borders. Windows often have a title, which can be found in the top border.
- Click On something means move the mouse pointer until it is over the thing and then press the left hand mouse button once.
- Double Click something means move the mouse pointer until it is over the thing and then press the left hand mouse button rapidly twice.
- Right Click means move the mouse pointer until it is over the thing and then press the right hand mouse button once.
- Some windows have a menu, which is a row of commands just under the title bar of the window. Typical menu items are File, Edit View etc. Each of these menu items, when clicked will display a further drop down menu. For example, the Edit menu will usually contain Copy, Cut and Paste. When we need to use one of these commands we will refer to it starting with the top level menu item then the lower level command. For example, if we say **Edit | Cut** this means click on the Edit menu item, then click on Cut.

This guide assumes that you understand what these conventions mean and that you have some basic familiarity with Windows (but not with Access 97). If you feel unsure about these basic ideas, you should gain some familiarity with windows, mice, icons, menus and buttons before starting the next chapter.

Exercise 1.2

Start up a Windows application that you are familiar with and make sure that you can identify and understand each of these features.

1.8. Summary

In this chapter we have covered a lot of details that you will need to bear in mind as you use the rest of the guide.

We spent some time defining some concepts that seem very familiar until you try to relate them to computer usage. Understanding data, information, database and database management systems is fundamental to your success with this guide and with this ECDL Module.

Access 97 is a relational database management system. We discussed the big idea that is at the heart of a relational database; that we store data in simple tables. A real database is composed of at least one and often many tables.

2

Getting Started

In this chapter you will learn how to

- *Start up and close down Access 97.*
- *Recognise the important features in an Access window.*
- *Open up an existing database.*
- *View a database.*
- *Modify a database record.*
- *Select and modify the toolbars.*
- *Use Access 97 Help.*
- *Save the database.*

In this chapter you will take your first steps to being competent with Access 97. We will concentrate initially on starting up and looking at a database and then shutting it down again correctly.

2.1. Starting Up Access 97

Access must be installed on your PC in order to make use of this guide. If you are unsure whether Access is installed, try the actions in the following sections. If you can't find the program, try re-installing the software, or seeking assistance.

The most certain way to start up Access is to click on the **Start** button at the bottom left hand corner of the screen, then click on **Programs**. You should see Microsoft Access listed, alongside its typical icon, a golden key. This will look something like Figure 2.1.

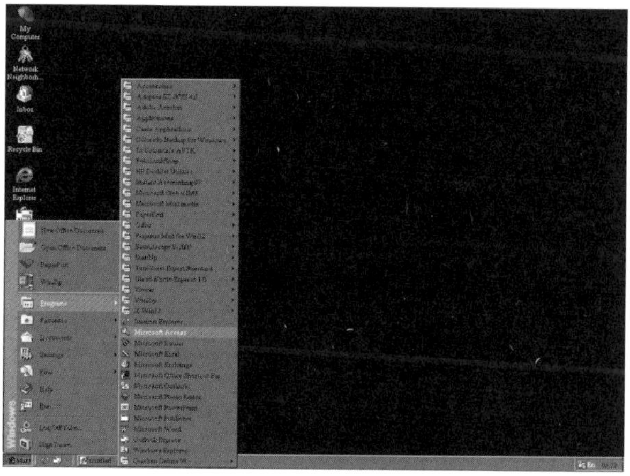

Figure 2.1 Starting Microsoft Access.

shortcut

It may be more convenient to set up Access as a shortcut on your screen, since you will be starting and stopping it many times during this guide.

Once Windows has started up Access you should see a window resembling Figure 2.2.

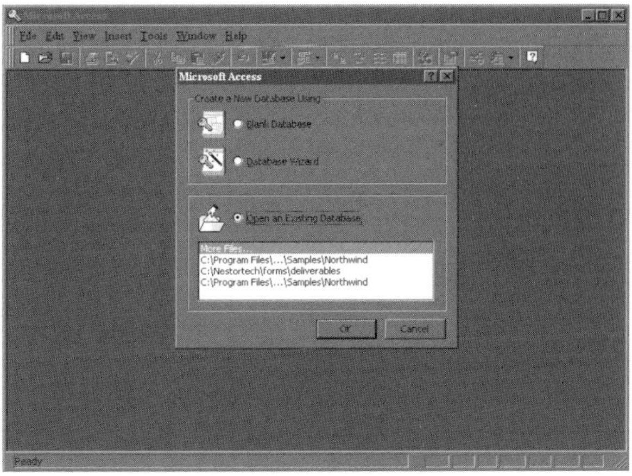

Figure 2.2 The opening screen for Microsoft Access.

At the moment we don't want to open an existing database, so simply close this window using the close button at the top right of the smaller window.

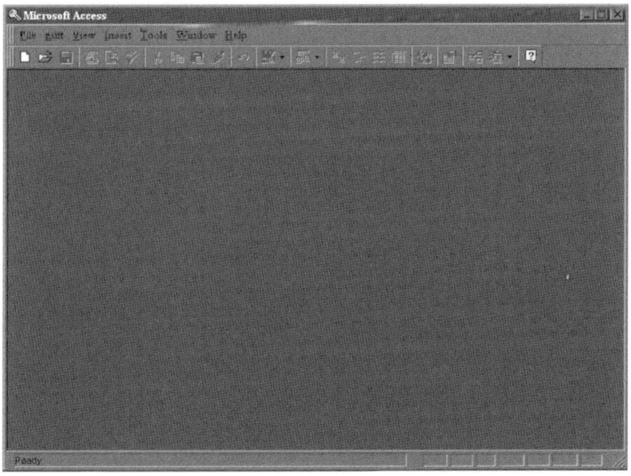

Figure 2.3 The Access window.

2.2. The Access Window

Take a look at the window shown in Figure 2.3; this is where we will spend most of the time in our exploration of Access. At the top of the window you will see the typical Windows menu bar just underneath the Access title bar. Most of the menu items will be familiar from other Windows applications:

- File is used to open new and existing databases, to close databases and to exit from Access. It also provides some Save functions, but these are not quite the same as those in other Office applications.
- Edit performs useful functions such as cutting and pasting things from one place to another.
- View is very important. It gives you different ways of looking at a database, particularly useful when you are building a new database.
- Insert might appear to be useful for adding data to your database, but its primary role is to help you to add new functions (such as reports and forms) to your database.
- Tools contains a collection of useful functions some of which, like spell check, may already be familiar. Some others are rather specialised and we will not use them in this guide.
- Window is all about manipulating the various different windows that you might have open at the same time. Access 97 allows you to have several windows open within the main application window, and the items in this menu allow you to organise them. This is exactly like all the other applications in Office 97.

caution!

Access is not like Word where you can have several documents open at once. The Access window only contains one database at a time.

- Help is another familiar menu item. We will use this quite frequently during the guide. Help behaves just like the help available for other Window applications.

Exercise 2.1

Explore the facilities provided by the menus by clicking on them and then selecting all the possible options. Note that some menus have further options, indicated by a small arrow. The range of options open to you will be limited at this stage, since you have not opened a database. Many of the options will be greyed out and not selectable, although you can still read them.

Once you have completed the exercise, exit from Access, using **File | Exit**.

2.3. Opening a Database

Now we have seen how Access looks without a live database, we can progress to trying it with a real database. We don't want to create a new database at this stage, we just want to look at a sample. Fortunately, Microsoft provides a sample database that is ideal for our needs. The database is called Northwind.mdb and will probably be located in a folder called Samples.

caution!

We want to keep the Northwind database safe so that we can always return to the original version. Other people may want to use the same PC after you so it is important that you return everything to the original state when you finish. An easy way to do this is to make a copy of the Northwind database. To do this use My Computer and browse to the folder that contains the Northwind database. Typically this is in C:\ProgramFiles\MicrosoftOffice\Office\Samples. Select the Northwind.mdb file, then Click on Edit | Copy and Edit | Paste. This will make a copy of the database. You can copy this back to the original Northwind.mdb any time to bring it back to the original condition.

To open the database, start up Access as we did before, but this time select **Open an Existing Database** and in response to the Open window, browse to select Northwind.mdb. You will see an opening graphic containing a lighthouse; click on **OK** to clear this and you should see a window similar to Figure 2.4.

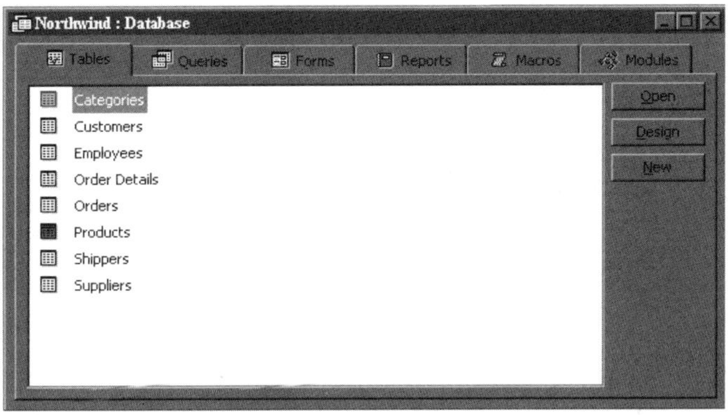

Figure 2.4 The Northwind database.

Notice that the Northwind database is shown as a tabbed window. There are tabs for Tables, Queries, Forms, Reports, Macros and Modules. We will not be concerned with Macros and Modules in this guide, but by the time you finish you will be familiar with the other four tabs.

Exercise 2.2

Repeat Exercise 2.1, navigating through all of the menu options. Don't change anything, just look at the range of options.

Did you notice that there is now a much wider range of options? This is because (as with all other Office applications) the menus change when you have opened a file, or in our case a database.

Make sure that the Tables tab is selected. You should see a list a tables displayed :

- Categories;
- Customers;
- Employees etc.

As we discussed in Chapter 1, a database typically consists of a number of linked tables, and the Northwind database has eight.

2.4. Viewing a Table

Take a look at the Employees table by double clicking on the table icon. The result should look like Figure 2.5

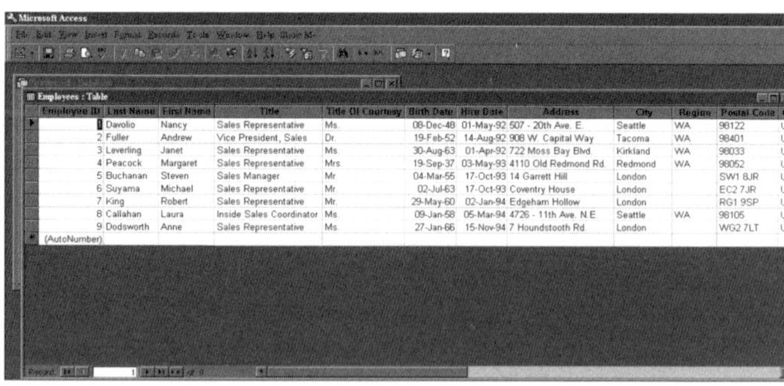

Figure 2.5 The Employees table.

The layout of the Table window may look familiar if you have ever used a spreadsheet such as Excel. Access shows tables in exactly the same way – a series of rows and columns. Each rectangle contains a single item of data. You can move around the table using the cursor key and the mouse. Your PC screen may not be large enough to display all the table at once. If this is the case, you can use the scroll bars at the side and bottom of the window to scroll it into view.

We need to introduce some new words at this stage to make sense of what Access will tell us.

definition

A data field or just field is the single fact or item of data in each of the rectangles in the table.

definition

A record is an alternative way of describing a row in a table.

caution!

Neither of these definitions would really stand up to close examination by a computer scientist, but they are acceptable for our purposes.

The bottom of the window contains some record navigation buttons. These use the same icons as a video-recorder. You can move up or down in the table one row (record) at a time, or skip directly to the first or last row. The record counter will show which record number you are currently viewing and how many records the table contains.

Exercise 2.3

Use the cursor keys to scroll from the left hand side of the table to the right hand side. Use the mouse to move from one row (record) to another. Use the video-recorder style buttons to move from one record to another and to the top and bottom of the table.

2.5. Modifying a Record

You can change the data in a table just by typing in the new data.

Exercise 2.4

Steven Buchanan has a new telephone extension number. Find the old number and change it to 3890.

2.6. Saving a Database

Now we have made a change we need to find out how to save these changes. This is very simple. Click on **File | Save** and the current database will be saved in the original file name. You should now appreciate why we made a copy of the original database file at the outset.

shortcut

In common with all the other Office applications, you can save time by using the key combination Ctrl+s to save the database. If you have not used such combinations before, the shorthand Ctrl+s means 'press the control key, then the s key then release both'. It is much faster than reaching for the mouse and going through the menus.

2.7. View Options

We have viewed a table, but what about the other parts of the database? We can look at these in just the same way that we viewed a table, through the Northwind tabbed window.

Exercise 2.5

Click on the **Queries** tab in the Northwind window. You should see a window containing fifteen different queries. Double click on **CurrentProductList**. Were you surprised with the result?

The queries look just like tables, but they aren't real tables containing real data. What you see is the result of running a query on a real table. This is subtle, but important; the result of a query on a table or tables is another table, but Access doesn't store that table as real data. It just works out what the table should look like every time we ask for it. This means that if we change the real tables, the results of a query on those tables will change automatically. This is a very powerful feature.

Now lets look at Forms. As you will have guessed, we can do this by clicking on the Forms tab.

Exercise 2.6

Click on the **Forms** tab and look for the **Employees** icon. Double click on this and you should see a form displayed. Navigate to the record for Steven Buchanan and check his extension number. What does this tell you about using a form?

A form is another way of looking at a table or more than one table. The simple spreadsheet approach is fine, but you would not want to use that all the time in a real system. A form is much more convenient. The answer to the exercise is that you could have changed the extension number using the form much more easily than you did in the raw table view. In case you were wondering, you can create forms on the tables that are produced by a query just as easily as if they were real tables.

Exercise 2.7

The form contains photographs. Go back to the **Table** view, open the **Employee** table and find out which column is used for the photos.
The photos are included in the **Photo** column. This is quite important; it tells us that we can store different types of data in a table. Pictures, text and numbers are just a few of the possibilities.

Finally we will take a look at Reports. You can reach these through the **Report** tab at the top of the Northwind window.

Exercise 2.8

Take a look at the **Summary of Sales by Year** report. What table did this data come from?

The data actually came from several tables and some of it was calculated, not stored in any table. This is typical of reports.

You have now seen all the main parts of the Northwind database, but we have not said anything about how we create tables, queries, forms and reports. We will take a quick look at this then return to the topic in detail later.

Make sure that you have closed any open forms, queries, tables or reports. Click on the **Tables** tab and select **Employees** with a single click. Now click on the **Design** button. You should see a window like that in Figure 2.6.

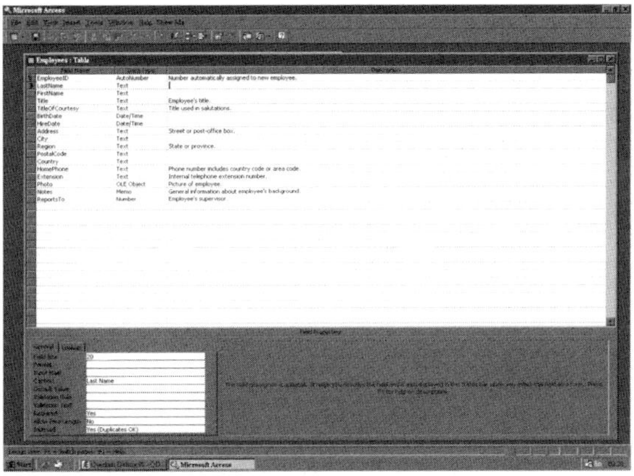

Figure 2.6 Table showing Field Name, Data Type and Description columns.

Look at the Field Name column. Each of these is a column in the Employee table; so this design view allows us to design a table by specifying what goes into each column.

The Data Type columns allow us to say what type of data is stored in each column of the table. Look down the column to see the various different types of data. These are fixed in advance as part of the design of Access, so you simply choose what you require.

The Description column allows us to describe what each column in the table is used for. Notice that some of the columns have no descriptions; this information is optional. Don't change anything, we are simply looking at this stage.

Now close the table and look at the Design views for the queries, forms and reports. In each case what you see in the design view is the set of tools used to construct or modify that type of object.

Normally we would not want people to be able to change the design of a database once it has been completed. This could lead to all kinds of confusion, or worse. In normal day-to-day use, people will not use the design views at all, and if you are the database designer you can stop them from seeing these. We will conclude this chapter by looking in more detail at the View menu.

Click on this now to look again at the options, shown in Figure 2.7.

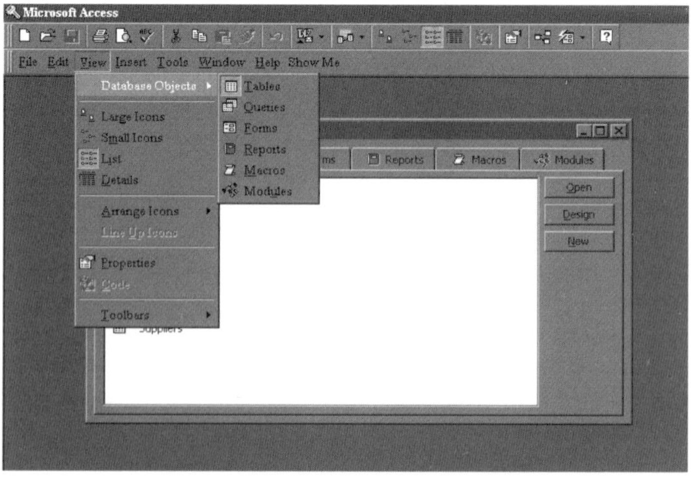

Figure 2.7 Options available in the View menu.

The database objects options simply select tables, queries etc in the same way as the tabs we used earlier.

Try using the Large icons, Small Icons, List etc. As you can see, these present a slightly different view of the objects in the database window. You can use whichever of these you prefer.

2.8. Selecting and Modifying Toolbars

View | Toolbars allows you to chose the toolbars displayed at the top of the window. There is a lot of choice in Access 97, but this is not immediately visible. To get a wider choice of toolbars, click on Customize. This will display a list of available toolbars (about twenty-two of them). You can choose any selection of these.

It is also possible to change the toolbars, adding or removing icons from them. Given the wide selection of available toolbars in Access, this should not be necessary for normal use.

2.9. Using Access 97 Help

Access Help follows the usual Office approach. Click on **Help** to see the available options. The Microsoft preferred tool is Microsoft Access Help. If you use this option, Access will open a small assistant window. This can assume a variety of different characters such as Einstein or a paper clip. You can call this up by clicking on Microsoft Access Help and then typing a question in the 'what would you like to do' window. This may help with your problem.

caution!

Then again, it may not. The purpose of the assistant is to be friendly and helpful, but it relies on understanding what you are asking and sometimes this doesn't work too well.

Once you have worked through even a small part of this guide you will probably prefer to get much more direct answers from Help. To do this, click on **Help | Contents** and **Index**. Contents is organised into a series of topics that you can choose, and is useful when you cannot remember (or do not know) how to carry out a specific task.

Sometimes you need to be even more specific. You can get help based on a particular word using the **Index** or **Find** options. These allow you to search for specific words or Help pages.

Exercise 2.9

Find out about toolbars and menus using the Index.

2.10. Summary

In this chapter we have seen how to start up Access 97, open, close and save databases and use various tools to view an existing database. We have seen that there are design views for all of the main database objects such as tables, queries, forms and reports. In the next chapter we will start to use these design views to create a new database.

3

Creating a Database

In this chapter you will learn how to

- *Define the rules for creating tables.*
- *Design and plan a database.*
- *Recognise the different types of data.*
- *Create an Access table.*
- *Use the commands to add a column to a table.*
- *Select and use Primary Keys.*
- *Set up an index on a table.*
- *Modify table design.*
- *Set up default values and display formats.*
- *Set up relationships between tables.*
- *Move through a table adding, deleting and modifying data.*

In the last chapter you gained some familiarity with Access 97, in particular its basic tools for viewing databases. Using a database is only part of the skill set that you will need. It is also important that you can create a new database from scratch, based on your understanding of a business requirement. This chapter is all about the process of designing a new database and implementing it using Access.

3.1. Designing Tables

We have seen that a database consists of one or more tables, but how do we decide what tables we need and what columns they should contain? This is a big issue that we will cover first.

A database is designed to solve a particular problem. It may be to do with business or perhaps personal data recording, but before we can make any progress we need to do some thinking about that problem.

The first stage is to decide which are the important things about which we need to record information. This is hard to do in an abstract fashion, so we will use a simple example.

Imagine you want to build a database to record information about your extensive CD collection. You keep all your CDs in a series of racks, and when necessary you buy a new rack. They are all the same design but of different sizes so they look nice in your living room. You sometimes forget which rack you have used to store a CD, so you decide to number the racks so that you can find a CD quickly. You want to be able to find which particular named tracks or songs are on which CD, so you need the database to record this. Similarly, you would like to record the artists or band that performs on each CD.

Exercise 3.1

Given this statement of your interests, try to produce a list of the main things that your database must be concerned with. Don't get bogged down in detail, just go for the important things. If you find it difficult, looking at an actual CD might help.

One answer to this exercise might be the following things:

- CD;
- Artist or Band;
- Track;
- Rack.

Now we need to decide what data we want to record for each of these different things. We will do the first two of these together, then you will try the third as an exercise. Your answers might be different; don't worry about this, there is a degree of subjectivity about the design based on what you think might be important.

The CD will have a title, and it will be produced by a record company. Since you are a really serious collector, you are also interested in the catalogue number. Notice that we have not included the tracks or the artist with the CD since these are different things.

The artist or band will have a name. You may also want to record their date of birth and some brief notes about their history, but only for those artists that really interest you. Date of birth sounds a little strange for a band or group, but there is no reason why you can't use this to actually mean the date that the group was first formed.

Exercise 3.2

Now try the same process for a track. Think of the data you would like to record about a particular track. Look at a real CD for inspiration. You might have decided that each track will have number, a name and a duration in minutes. This is almost always provided on the sleeve notes.

The rack is simple. All we need is its rack number and perhaps the number of CDs that it can store so we can quickly see when it is becoming full.

To summarise: we have the following things that we want to store and the most important data fields for each:

CD
- Title
- Record Company
- Catalogue number

Artist
- Name
- Date of Birth
- History

Track
- Number
- Name
- Duration

Rack
- Number
- Capacity

3.2. Derived Data

You might want to know the total number of minutes of recording on a CD. We have not included this data in our design but it could be added to the CD table. We will not do that because it would be a poor design decision. The total play time of a CD is derivable data; that is, it can be calculated by adding together all the play lengths of all the tracks on the CD. Except under some very special conditions, you should never include such derivable data in your tables. There are a two main reasons for this:

1. You should aim to store a fact about something in one place and in one way only. Storing it in two ways means that there is the potential for them to disagree, which could result in inconsistent information being produced from your database.

2. Storing derivable data wastes space. Admittedly this is minimal in this case, but in a big database it can be an important factor.
You might think that calculating the total play time would take a significant amount of time. This is not really true; the calculation would be almost instantaneous, but finding all the track records will take a little longer. Even though there might be a small penalty in speed, this is worth accepting, knowing that the database can't give inconsistent information.

3.3. Primary Keys

Each thing that we decide to store in database needs to be identifiable in a reliable manner. The next stage is to decide on the best way to identify each of the four things that we have decided are important. We would really like to use one of the data fields that we have selected, but it is important that we choose something that is unique and will remain so for ever.

For example, we might think that we could identify every CD by means of its Name, but that would lead us into difficulty. There are dozens of recordings of each of the Beethoven symphonies, even multiple recordings by the same orchestra so the title would not be enough to identify any one of them. We may only have one of these recordings at the moment, but we might well buy a second one at some future date. A much better choice would be the catalogue number, since the recording companies work hard to ensure that these are truly unique – it makes their life easier.

Artist should be easier, since the artist's or band's name should be enough to uniquely identify them. But further thought shows that this is not always true – there is at least one famous example of a singer who quite deliberately changed his name. There is another problem with an artist's name as an identifier, because we will need to spell it correctly and consistently every time we enter the data. If we don't, we will not get correct results when we try to get information from the database at a later stage. Yet another consideration is that where possible it is better to make the identifier short and numeric; the database will usually work faster like that. All of these factors suggest that the Artist's name would work as an identifier, but is not the best choice. In this case an Artist Number, unique for every Artist would be a better choice.

shortcut

This situation occurs fairly frequently. Access 97 provides a special kind of number that is good for making identifiers in these situations. The number is increased by one every time we add a row to the database, so Access guarantees that it is always unique.

Track appears to be simple – we could use the track number. A little thought shows that this doesn't really work. Every CD will have a track 1 on it, so Track Number is not unique. We could use the Track Name, but that is not guaranteed to be unique. It is possible that there might be two entirely different CDs with the same name for a track. In fact this is likely to happen fairly frequently because Artists tend to cover (produce their own versions) of each other's tracks. It also suffers from the same problem as the Artist Name, it is potentially too long and difficult to keep typing. Even the combination of track number and name is not guaranteed to be unique. There is an obvious way to fix this problem, and that is to use the CD catalogue number, in combination with the Track Number. This absolutely guarantees that we can uniquely identify each track. Our identifier will therefore be a combination of two fields.

For Rack we can use the rack number. This has no problems, especially as we can ensure that every time we buy a new rack, we can give it a new, unique label.

The technical term for the unique identifiers we have found is a Primary Key. To record our choices we can underline the Primary Key, so our design to this point is:

CD
- Title
- Record Company
- Catalogue Number

Artist
- Artist Number
- Name
- Date of Birth(DOB)
- History

Track
- Catalogue Number
- Track Number
- Name
- Duration

Rack
- Rack Number
- Capacity

3.4. Types of Data

Now we need decide what type of data we will require for each of the data fields. As we will find later, there are a lot of possibilities, but for the present we will use only the basic types that Access provides. These are:

1. Text – used for fields that contain alphabetic data, usually a single word or a short phrase.

2. Memo – Used for much larger amounts of textual data, perhaps a description of something.

3. Number – Used for numbers. If you think you might need to do sums with a data field, it should use the Number data type.

4. Date/Time – If you want to store dates and/or time, use this data type. Access will recognise the dates and allow you to do useful date-related things with them.

5. Currency – Use this data type when you want to store amounts of money.

6. AutoNumber – This is useful when we want Access to create a series of numbers that automatically increase whenever we add a new record.

Auto Number is exactly what we need to make an identifier for the Artist table.

7. Yes/No – Sometimes we just want to store information that can only have one of two possible values. For example, we might want to store a person's gender. This can only be Male or Female.

Exercise 3.3

Decide on the most appropriate data types for our CD database design, recording the type alongside each field.

A reasonable answer would be:

CD		
	Title	Text
	Record Company	Text
	Catalogue Number	Text
Artist		
	Artist Number	AutoNumber
	Name	Text
	Date of Birth (DOB)	Date/Time
	History	Memo
Track		
	Catalogue Number	Text
	Number	Number
	Name	Text
	Duration	Number
Rack		
	Number	Number
	Capacity	Number

Notice that we have used memo for history. This is because sometimes we may want to write a lot of notes and at other times nothing at all. Memo is a good choice for this type of situation.

There is a final check that we should carry out on our database design before we are ready to start working with Access.

Look at each of the things that you have decided are important (CD Artist etc.) and decide whether the whole of the Primary Key decides uniquely (on its own) the values of all the other fields, and that none of the other fields can do this.

- For example, if we know the CD catalogue number, is there only one possible CD Name and Record Company? The answer is clearly yes.
- Can we tell unambiguously what the CD Name is if we only know the Record Company? The answer is clearly no, only the Primary Key determines the CD name.

You should apply this test to all of the things that you have identified. If you find something that does not satisfy the test, then take a close look at your design. Probably you have two separate things mixed together. Try to separate them out.

This test may seem rather mysterious, but it is important. Passing the test means that your database design should work well and not give you any strange results. Designs that don't pass the test could eventually cause surprising effects or lose data altogether.

information

The process we have just described is technically described as normalisation and is an essential part of the process of designing a database. There is a great deal more to this process than we have described here, but you can gain most of the benefits by applying the tests described. Another way of stating the tests for normalisation is a variation on the oath sworn by witnesses in court: "Does every field depend on the Primary Key, the whole of the Primary Key and nothing but the Primary Key?"

3.5. Indexes

An index helps Access to find rows in a table much more quickly. We use indexes all the time in normal life without thinking about them very much. For example, this book has an index that allows you to find pages that contain specific topic words. To use the index, you scan through it until you find the word then open the book at the page number shown. We can scan the index quickly because it is always in alphabetic order. Just consider the alternative; without an index, you would have to read through large parts of the text to find where a topic was covered. In the extreme you might have to read a whole book just to find out what a particular small topic was all about.

You don't have to define any indexes when you first design a database. You can add them later if you really need them. Access, like any good relational database will deliver results whether or not you define any additional indexes. You might think that if indexes speed up the retrieval of data from the database, we would obviously set up indexes on every field. Unfortunately, it isn't as simple as that because indexes on the wrong fields can actually slow things down a lot and greatly increase the size of the database. This is because keeping the indexes up to date absorbs computer power, and requires extra data, sometimes very significantly.

The best approach to adopt, at least until you have more experience with databases is to follow these guidelines:

- Only set up indexes on fields that hold text, numbers, currency or dates.
- Only set up indexes on fields that will be used a lot.
- Only set up indexes on fields that will contain a lot of different values.
- If in doubt don't set up an index, unless and until you are sure that your database isn't working quickly enough.

Access automatically sets up indexes on Primary Keys for you. This makes sense because Primary Keys have different values in every row, are used a lot and are usually numbers, dates or short text fields.

3.6. Access Database Wizards

Access 97, (and other database management systems) supplies you with some sample database designs that you can use without having to go through the processes that we have described above. To use these you start Access in the normal way, but when you see the Microsoft Access window select Database Wizard. Access will then display a list of database templates. If you select one of these, Access will take you through a series of windows in which you can make various choices about the layout of the database.

Database Wizards are ideal if your requirements are met by the supplied templates. Unfortunately the templates are rarely an exact fit, so you will either have to compromise your requirements or modify the database design. We will cover such modifications later in the chapter, but for the present we will assume that you want to build a database that meets your exact requirements.

information

There is a Music Collection database in the standard set of samples. The design is slightly different to the one we are working with. When we have finished you can compare your results with the one created by the Database Wizard.

3.7. The Table Design Toolbar

Access provides a set of toolbars that are tailored to match all the major design tasks. We will describe each of these toolbars as we need them.

Most of the Access toolbars come in pairs. Typically the first of these provides all the major tools you will need to create and change something like a table, and its matching pair is intended to help you use the object you have created (such as a table). You can flip between the deign view and the user view with a special button. This is really useful when you are learning Access since you can try out a change in the design view then immediately flip to the other view to check your changes.

Figure 3.1 shows the toolbars that are available for table design. Access will normally display the toolbars when you work with a table, but if for any reason they are not visible, click on **View | Toolbars** and select the toolbar you need.

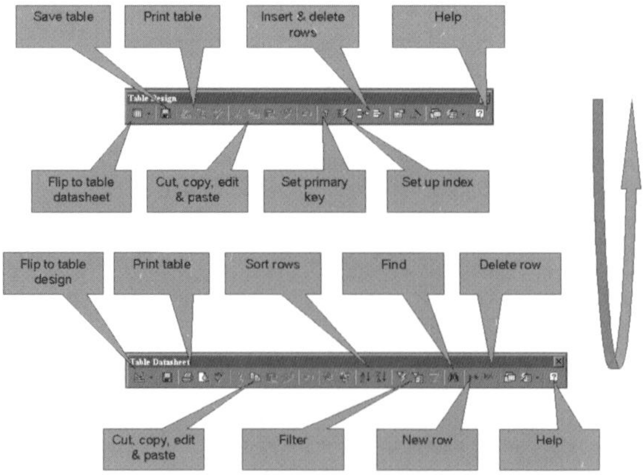

Figure 3.1 Toolbars available for table design.

ECDL

The table design toolbar has all the usual save, print, cut, copy and paste buttons. There are also some special purpose buttons that we will use during this chapter and that you should look out for:

- Set Primary Key is used to tell Access which column or columns are the Primary Key for the table.
- Set up index is used to define which columns should have an index to speed up retrieval of data.
- Flip to datasheet moves you from the table design view to the table datasheet view.

The table datasheet toolbar also has some special purpose buttons:

- Sort rows allows you to sort the rows into a different sequence.
- Find helps you to find a particular example of a number or a word within a table.
- Filter helps you by displaying only those rows that meet a particular requirement. This is very useful with big tables.

Note that help is available on both these toolbars (and on every other toolbar).

3.8. Creating Tables

The first task in implementing our database design in Access is to set up a new blank database.

Start up Access 97, and then select **Blank Database** and click **OK**. This will lead to the **File New Database** window shown in Figure 3.2.

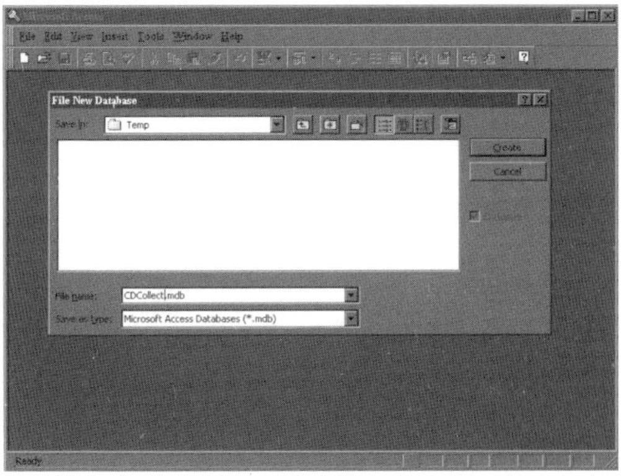

Figure 3.2 The File New Database window.

Choose a suitable name for your database and click on **Create**. We will call our CD database *CDCollect.mdb*. The mdb extension is the standard Microsoft file ending for Access databases in the same way that doc is used for Word documents.

You will next see the familiar Database window, with CDCollect in the title bar. We are ready to start creating tables. Each of the things that we decided were important in our design will become a table and each of the fields will be a column. We will start with CD. Click on **New** and you will see the window shown in Figure 3.3.

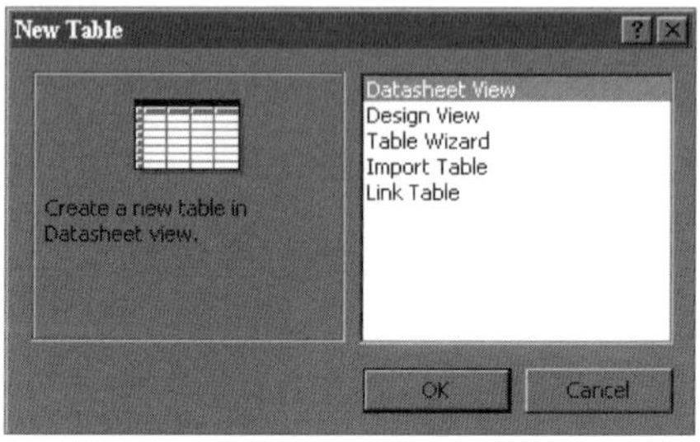

Figure 3.3 Creating a new table.

Note that there is a Table Wizard that can help you create some standard types of table, but just as with the Database Wizard, these do not match our requirements exactly, so we will use the **Design View** and click **OK**. This will result in a blank Table Design window similar to that shown in Figure 3.4. Access thoughtfully provides a Table Design toolbar as well.

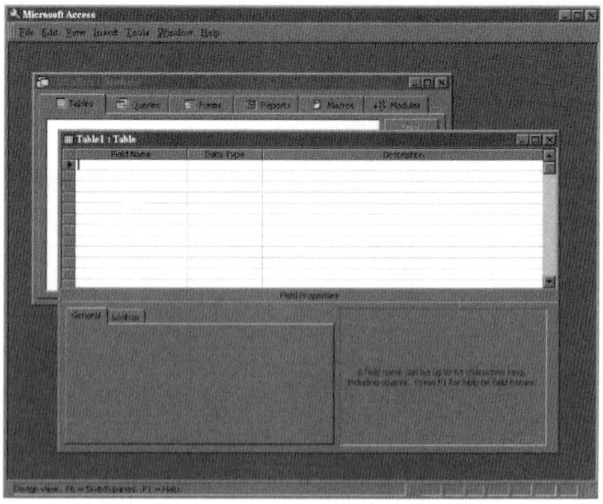

Figure 3.4 A blank Table Design window.

3.9. Adding Fields

Type in the first field name, which is *Name*, in the first row of the table, then press the Tab key to move on to the next column, **Data Type**.

shortcut

The tab key is a quick way to move between fields in many different situations.

Notice that Access provides a drop down list to choose the data type, so click on the **arrow** and select **Text**. Tab on to the next column and type in a description of this field; something like: *The Name of the CD*. Press Tab again to go to the next row and enter the remaining data fields. Finally, we need to tell Access which of our fields is the Primary Key. This is the underlined field in our design. Select the **Catalogue Number** field then click on the **Primary Key button** on the **Table Design** toolbar. This button looks like a small key. Access will show the Primary Key by inserting a small picture of a key just to the left of Catalogue Number.

You should finish up with something that looks like Figure 3.5

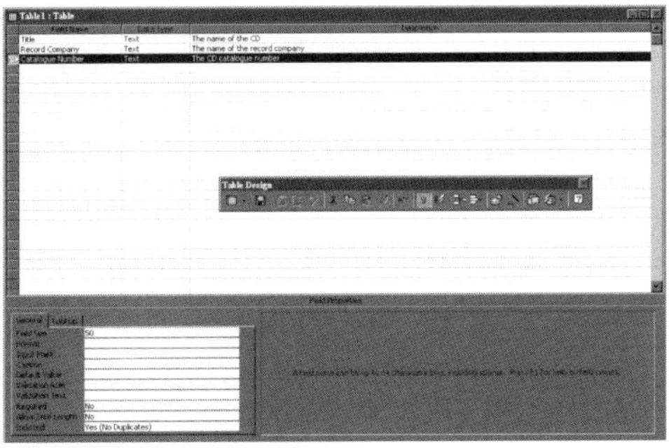

Figure 3.5 The result of an initial table design.

Now we need to save the table design. The simplest way to do this is using the save button on the Table Design toolbar (see Figure 3.1), with the floppy disk icon. When you click on this, Access will prompt you for a table name. The name of this table is *CD*, so type that in and click on **OK**. You can now close the Table window by clicking the close button in the top right hand corner. This will bring you back to the Database window.

Set up the other tables in just the same way as for the CD table.

3.10. More Data Types

We saw earlier that Access recognises seven basic types of data:

Text, Memo, Number, Date/Time, Currency, AutoNumber and Yes/No.

Two of these types, Number and Date/Time come in a variety of different forms. You need to choose the most appropriate for your design.

One of the reasons why Access provides all this choice is that storing data requires disk space. Some forms of Numbers and Dates require a lot more space than others, so there is a big advantage in choosing the most economical type of format for your needs.

Another reason why Access provides different types of Numbers is that there really are different types of numbers in everyday use.

d definition

Integers are used for counting whole things that never come in fractional parts.

d definition

Floating point numbers are used for measuring things that can change smoothly in value and have a decimal point.

! caution!

This may seem a rather artificial distinction, but it does matter. Using the wrong type of number can lead to silly answers or the loss of data.

Here are some examples of the use of different types of numbers:

- Integers would be used for counting people, CDs, books and cars. 0.35 people does not make sense, neither would 0.76 of a car, but 3 students and 25 cars with no decimal points does seem reasonable.
- We measure weight in kilograms, so a person might weigh 70.42 kilograms. We do not think of weight as being limited to whole numbers of kilos, so we would naturally use floating-point numbers to record weight.

In addition to dividing numbers into integer and floating point, Access also has numbers that are capable of storing big values with a lot of accuracy and numbers that can only store small numbers with limited accuracy. Each of these different types of number has a different name. These are all shown in Figure 3.6.

Name	Type	Decimal Places	Range
Byte	Integer	None	0 to 255
Integer	Integer	None	-32678 to 32767
Long Integer	Integer	None	Very large
Single	Float	7	Typical numbers
Double	Float	15	Enormous

Figure 3.6 The different types of numbers used by Access.

You should first decide whether you need an integer or a floating-point number. Then choose the number with the smallest range that you are quite certain will be able to hold the biggest possible value that the data field could ever have.

caution!

If you get this wrong, and choose a number type that is too small, Access will give you a warning when you try to enter a larger number in it, and will then store the number effectively as zero, so you will lose that data completely. This loss can also have a knock-on effect on other things that you might want to use that number for, such as calculations. If you are unsure, choose a bigger number type.

3.11. Choosing Field Options

Once you have some basic tables defined, you should start adding some more detail to your fields. You may have noticed that there are a number of additional options at the bottom of the Table Design window. These add a great deal to the usefulness of the database so you should use them where appropriate. The additional options are:

- Field Size: Maximum length of the field measured in characters, or the selection of the number types that we have just discussed.

- Format: Allows you to decide how the field will be displayed
- Input Mask: Mask might seem a rather mysterious term, but it simply means the things that will be valid when data is entered in the field. This is very important because specifying an input mask helps to ensure that only valid data is added to the database.
- Caption: This is a label that can be used in a form or a report; again it is useful to define this.
- Default Value: A value that will be automatically supplied when a new record is created, unless data is entered for this field.
- Validation Rule: A means of ensuring that only correct data can be entered. These can become very sophisticated, but we will only consider simple validation rules.
- Validation Text: You can enter some text here that will prompt a user for what type of data must be entered.
- Required: Some fields must always be filled with data. Others may not require an entry in every record. If a field is marked as Required = yes, it must have data entered.
- Allow Zero Length: This allows a text field to have no characters in it.
- Indexed: Defines whether or not an index is created on this field.

You can set up an index simply by selecting Yes. You must choose whether duplicate values will be allowed for this field.

Exercise 3.6

Access always sets up an index for the Primary Key with no duplicates allowed. Why do you think this is so? If you are unsure, revise Section 3.3.

If you look at Artist table and the Name field you will see that some of these Properties are already set, but they are not really appropriate for our design. We will correct or add all the useful details, then you can do the same for the other tables and fields.

- The field size is probably set to 50 characters. This is a little generous, but we will leave it alone, since it is possible that a band name might approach this number of characters. Generally, the number of characters should be kept as small as possible without limiting the typical use of the field.
- Format and Input Masks are currently not set, and since there is no real pattern to the name of an artist or band there is no advantage in specifying a format in this case.
- Captions is useful, so we will enter 'Artist/Band'
- There is no sensible Default Value, Validation Rule or Validation Text for this field, so we will not enter this data.
- We will always require an artist or band name so we will mark this field as required. Similarly, we don't want to allow the field to contain no characters, so we will disallow zero length.

We will carry through the same process for the DOB field.

- Format does not show a length of field, because Access already knows that this is a date field. If you click on the Format field you will see a range of possible date formats. These are:

  1. General Date
  2. Long Date
  3. Medium Date
  4. Short Date
  5. Long Time
  6. Medium Time
  7. Short Time

  We don't need a really accurate date/time, so Short Date is a suitable choice.

- Input Mask also presents options that are suitable for a date field. Click on the drop down arrow to display these and choose. Make sure that the date format matches your local country standards, otherwise users will be able to enter data in a familiar formats. You will be guided through your choice of an Input Mask by a small Wizard, which is very useful in this case.
- We will add a suitable Caption as before, but will not bother with a Default Value, a Validation Rule or Validation Text.
- We do not require data to be entered in this field (some singers may be coy about their age!), nor do we need an index.

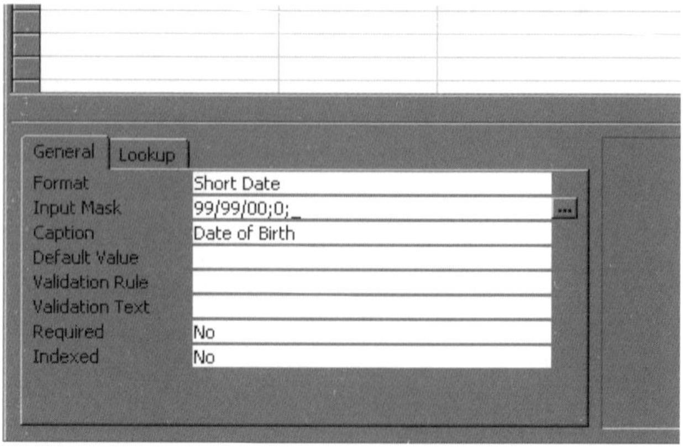

Figure 3.7 Choosing the field options for Date of Birth.

Exercise 3.7

Now carry out the same process for all the other fields in your CD database.

You should not have had any major problems completing the exercise, but if you later decide that you need to change anything, you can simply go back to the Design View for that table and alter it.

3.12. Setting Up Relationships

As we saw in Chapter 1, most databases store data about more than one thing, and there is useful information in the way those things are related to each other.

Take our CD database as an example. We now have tables for CDs, artists, racks and tracks, but these are all entirely separate. This does not actually tell us a great deal about our collection. We cannot, for example say which Artists perform on which CDs, nor can we find out where we have put a particular CD because there are no connections at all between these different types of records. We have to add those connections to our database.

To do this we need some further analysis of our design. We need to ask the following question of the things in our database.

- How many of this thing could be related to some other thing?

An example will make this obscure question more understandable.

- How many CDs could an artist be a performer on? Answer: at least one and possibly a lot.

How many artists could appear on a single CD? Strictly speaking the answer could be several, but this is unusual. For our collection we will assume that only one artist or band performs on a CD. If we really do have a collection of artists, we will call the artist "Various Artists".

Expressing this in database terms, One Artist is related to Many CDs, but any single CD has only one Artist.

caution!

You must use some judgement about defining relationships. In a more extensive database design, you could define an enormous number of relationships, most of which would be irrelevant to your application. It is important that you keep in mind the questions that you will want to ask of your database and define the relationships that are essential for that purpose.

To make this relationship clear to Access, we need to add some details to the database.

Exercise 3.8

First we need to add the Primary Key from the 'One' side of the relationship, (in this case Artist) to the 'Many' side (CD).This is shown in Figure 3.8

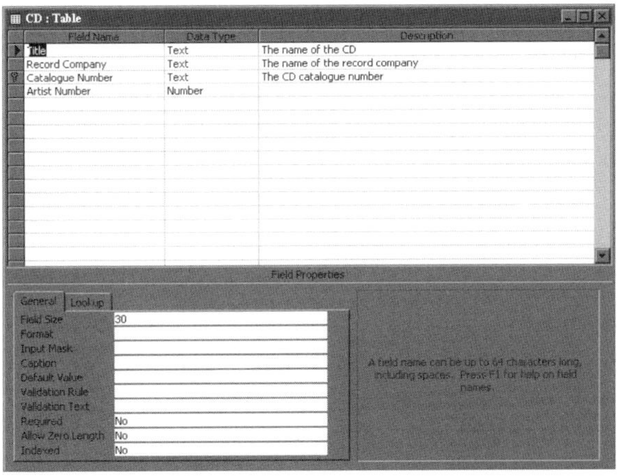

Figure 3.8 Adding the Primary Key from the 'One' side to the 'Many' side.

Notice that we don't have to use exactly the same name for the added field, In fact it is probably better in this case to spell out the name as we have done, so there is no confusion. Notice also that the Artist Name field has been set to Required yes, meaning that we must always say what band or artist performs on a CD.

Now we need to connect these matching fields so that Access knows that the Name field in Artist is connected to the Artist Name field in CD.

To do this you should click on **Tools | Relationships** from the main Access menu. This will display a window called **Show Table**, which will contain the names of all the tables you have defined so far. Click on each table in turn and click on **Add**. A new small window representing each table will appear, so your screen will look like Figure 3.9

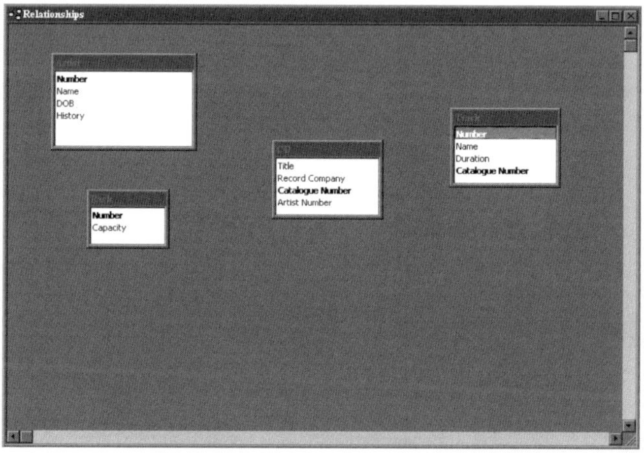

Figure 3.9 Preparing to connect matching fields.

You may need to resize some of the windows and move them around to get a tidy layout. Notice that Access has provided us with a new toolbar.

To make the connection, Click on the Primary Key on the One side of the relationship (Name) and drag it to the corresponding field on the Many side Artist Name. You will see the mouse cursor change shape as you do this and a new window will appear entitled Relationships. This is used to define the nature of the relationship. Most of the work is already done for you, but one important additional action is to select the **Enforce Relational Integrity** box. This will make Access ensure that the relationship you have defined will always be maintained, so the database will not let you enter a new CD without saying who the artist is.

caution!

After you have gained some further experience with databases, you may decide not to enforce 'Relational Integrity' but for the present you should let Access handle this for you. The result of this will be a Relationships window that looks like Figure 3.10.

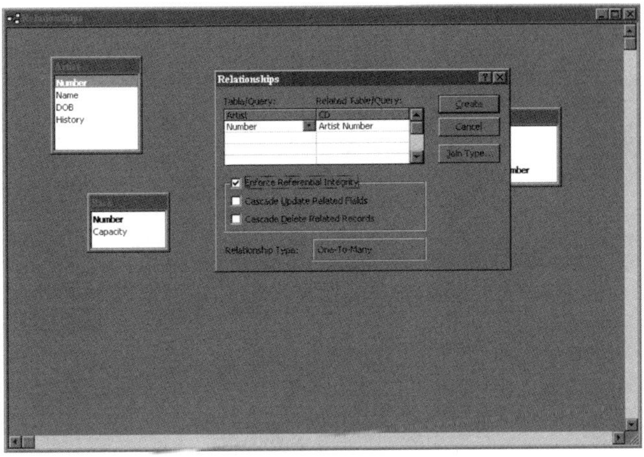

Figure 3.10 Example of a Relationships window.

Click the **Create** button to complete the process of establishing the link between the tables. The link will be shown as line joining the appropriate fields, with a figure 1 adjacent to the Artist table and ∞ (infinity) at the other end of the link. This is a visual cue to remind you that this is a one to many relationship between Artist and CD.

Now complete your analysis of the CD collection database design to decide what other relationships need to be represented, and which end of each relationship is 'One' and which is 'Many'

There are two more relationships:

- One CD can have Many Tracks;
- One Rack can contain Many CDs.

caution!

When you get to defining the relationship between CD and Track, you will find that you already have the Primary Key of CD as a field in Track, so you don't need to add it again. This helps to confirm that we made a good choice at an earlier stage.

Exercise 3.9

Add these Relationships to your Access database, then rearrange the table windows so that it looks tidy.

The actual arrangement of the tables in the Relationship window does not matter. You should have noticed that as you drag the tables around, the links remain connected. The arrangement in Figure 3.11 shows how it might look, but you may have used different names for the additional fields in CD.

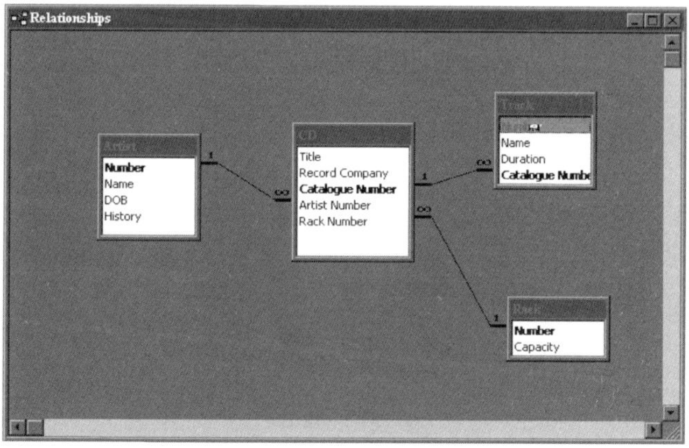

Figure 3.11 Your Relationship window should look something like this.

3.13. Entering Data in a Table

Now we have a working database we should test it by entering some data in the tables. This will serve two purposes;

- We will explore the details of data entry into tables, particularly where these tables are related.
- We can test the design of the CD database.

ECDL

We will use the simple Datasheet View that we first encountered in Chapter 2, but this time we will be working with the CDCollect database.

Exercise 3.10

Start from the CDCollect:Database window. Select the CD icon and click on Open to open this table in the Datasheet view.

The result should look like Figure 3.12.

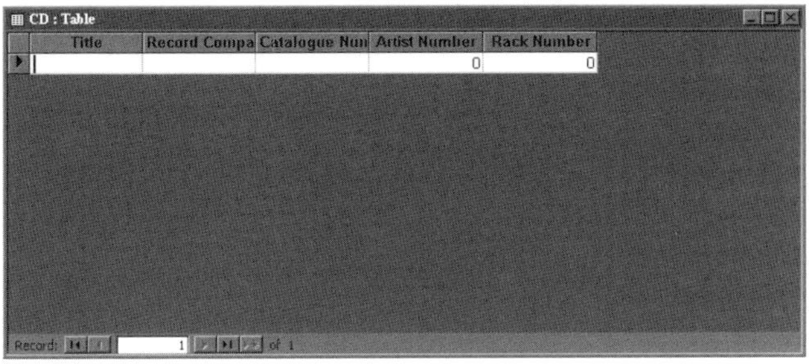

Figure 3.12 Opening table in the Datasheet view.

You can immediately see that we need to make some changes to the layout in order to make data entry easy. The problem is that the columns have a uniform width, and in two cases, we cannot read the titles at the top of the columns.

The Datasheet View behaves in a similar way to a spreadsheet. We can drag the column boundaries to enlarge the column.

To resize a column, move the mouse cursor until it lies on the title area of the column on the vertical column boundary. At this point the cursor will change shape to a double-headed arrow. Press down the left hand mouse button and drag the column boundary to the required position.

Resize all the columns so that they are a sensible width for data entry. Since the first three fields are all fairly large, you will not be able to make the columns the full width of the fields, but choose a comfortable size.

Now we will add some real data to the database.

Exercise 3.11

The data we will use is for the following CD, Artist and Rack.

Title :	Blood On The Tracks
Record Company:	Columbia
Catalogue Number:	COL 4678422
Artist Name:	Bob Dylan
DOB:	24 May 1941
History:	Born Robert Allen Zimmerman, Duluth Minnesota. First record, 1962. Serious motorcycle accident 29 July 1966. First movie part in Pat Garrett and Billy the Kid.
Rack Number:	8, which can store 100 CDs

Tracks:

1	Tangled Up In Blue	5.66
2	Simple Twist of Fate	4.30
3	You're a Big Girl Now	4.60
4	Idiot Wind	7.90
5	You're Gonna Make Me Lonesome When You Go	2.90
6	Meet Me In The Morning	4.32
7	Lily, Rosemary And The Jack Of Hearts	8.83
8	If You See Her, Say Hello	4.77
9	Shelter From The Storm	4.98
10	Buckets Of Rain	3.48

Enter the data for this CD, starting with the CD table. If you encounter any problems, make a note of the messages from Access and try to work out what has gone wrong.

You probably got a message stating that: "You can't add or change a record because a related record is required in table Artist" The Help button will provide a more detailed explanation.

This tells you that you can't add a record to the Many side of relationship until the matching record exists on the One side of the relationship. Translating this into simpler language, Access 97 will not let you create a database record for a CD without first entering the data for the Artist. A similar problem exists for the Rack. This problem exists because we chose to enforce 'referential integrity' when we set up the relationships between tables. If you try to get around this problem by ignoring the messages, you will receive further messages, and finally Access 97 will say that it cannot save your changes.

Exercise 3.12

The simplest way round this problem is to enter the data in the following order:

1. Artist
2. Rack
3. CD
4. Track

This fills all the tables on the One side of each relationship before the Many side.

Try entering the data using this sequence. Make a note of anything that you found difficult, or clumsy

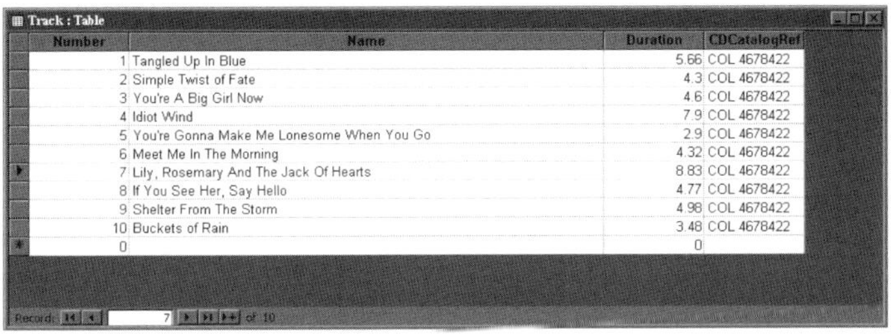

Track : Table

Number	Name	Duration	CDCatalogRef
1	Tangled Up In Blue	5.66	COL 4678422
2	Simple Twist of Fate	4.3	COL 4678422
3	You're A Big Girl Now	4.6	COL 4678422
4	Idiot Wind	7.9	COL 4678422
5	You're Gonna Make Me Lonesome When You Go	2.9	COL 4678422
6	Meet Me In The Morning	4.32	COL 4678422
7	Lily, Rosemary And The Jack Of Hearts	8.83	COL 4678422
8	If You See Her, Say Hello	4.77	COL 4678422
9	Shelter From The Storm	4.98	COL 4678422
10	Buckets of Rain	3.48	COL 4678422
0		0	

Record: 7 of 10

Figure 3.13 The completed Track table should look like this.

Figure 3.13 shows what the Track table should look like when you have finished. You may have found that entering the Track data was a little laborious and wondered whether it was strictly necessary to provide some of the data.

For example, why do we have enter the track number in each case? Surely Access 97 knows that if we enter the tracks in sequence the track numbers should follow that sequence?

The answer to this is rather important. Access 97 is a relational database, and with any relational database, the sequence or order of rows in a table is not relevant and may not be maintained by the database. You cannot rely on being able to obtain the track number from the sequence of rows in the table, so we need to enter it.

Why do we need to keep entering the Catalogue number for each record? Just because you entered all these records together does not mean that Access 97 associates them automatically with the same CD; the Catalogue number is essential for each record.

shortcut

You can significantly reduce the effort and potential for error when entering the same data again and again by using the clipboard. Type in the first value, then select the entry by dragging the cursor though it. Click on Edit | Copy to copy it to the clipboard. Now every time you need to enter that data, you can type Shift/Insert to insert a copy.

Exercise 3.13

Now enter the data for the following CD, using what you have learnt. The Artist data is not repeated, since it is the same as before.

Title :	Blonde on Blonde
Record Company:	CBS
Catalogue Number:	CDCBS 22130
Artist Name:	Bob Dylan
Rack Number;	6, which can store 75 CDs

Tracks:

1	Rainy Day Women Nos 12 & 35	4.58
2	Pledging My Time	3.72
3	Visions Of Johanna	7.50
4	One Of Us Must Know (Sooner Or Later)	4.92
5	I Want You	3.11
6	Stuck Inside Of Mobile With The Memphis Blues Again	7.07
7	Leopard-Skin Pill Box Hat	3.85
8	Just Like A Woman	4.68
9	Most Likely You Go Your Way And I'll Go Mine	3.24
10	Temporary Like Achilles	4.82
11	Absolutely Sweetmarie	4.78
12	4TH Time Around	4.46
13	Obviously 5 Believers	3.52
14	Sad Eyed lady Of The Lowlands	10.75

Take a look at the tables after you have entered the data. You will find that we have made a small error in the table design. One of the tracks has such a long name that it has exceeded the size of the field that we allocated. We can correct this error quite simply by closing the table and re-opening it in **Design View**. We can change the **Field size** to 55 characters, solving the problem. Close the **Design View** and then re-open the table in **Datasheet view** and correct the name that was truncated. This kind of change can be made to the table design after data has been entered in the table.

Figure 3.14 shows how the tables should look after all these changes. Don't bother arranging your table windows like this, just check them one by one.

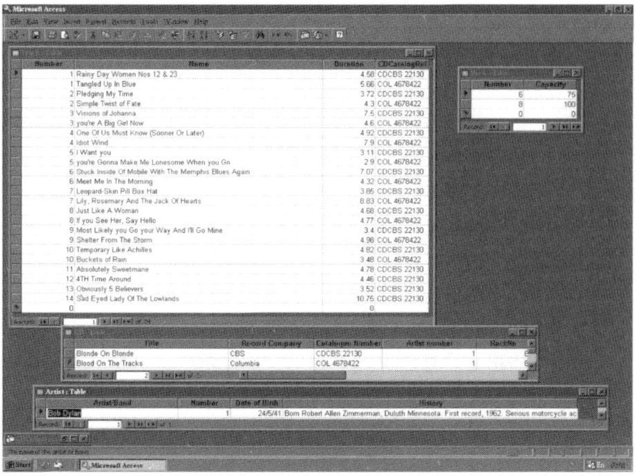

Figure 3.14 Tables resulting from the changes made.

caution!

> **Access 97 is very forgiving of this kind of change, but there are some changes that will cause your existing data to become invalid, so be cautious when making design alterations.**

3.14. Deleting Data in a Table

Deleting a row from a table is easy. Select the record that you wish to delete by clicking at the far left hand side of the row as you see it in the Datasheet View. The whole row will go black indicating its selection. You can now use the Del key on the keyboard or the **Edit | Delete Record** menu item to delete the row. Access 97 will show you a warning telling you that "You are about to delete one record(s)". If you click **Yes**, the record will be deleted and you will not be able to undo this action. This message gives you a useful clue that you can delete several rows at the same time with this method if you wish.

caution!

> **We found that Access 97 maintains relational integrity when we add new records. The same is true when we delete records. If you try to delete a record that is at the One end of a One to Many relationship, Access 97 will not let you. It will display a warning with a Help button to give you further guidance.**

It is also possible to delete records using forms, and this is the typical way that users will carry out this action.

3.15. Sorting Table Data

You probably notice that the Track table no longer displays the tracks in the order they were entered. You can change the order in which the rows of a table are displayed to make it easy to work with the data.

caution!

Changing the ordering of the rows in a table has no effect on any applications, queries, reports or forms that you may use. Remember, relational databases do not make any use of the sequence of the rows in a table.

Exercise 3.15

We might want the tracks displayed in alphabetical order. Left click on the **Name title** at the top of the column. The whole of the column will be highlighted. Now right click the mouse. You will see the **Sort Ascending** and **Sort Descending** options. Sort Ascending puts the As at the top and the Zs at the bottom of the column. If you look closely at the menu icons, you will see this represented graphically. We will select the Ascending option. Re-sort the table based on Track Number, then re-sort again on CDCatalogRef. Did you get the result you expected?

3.16. Re-Arranging Table Columns

The order of the columns in a table Datasheet can be changed quite simply. This is purely a cosmetic change. Relational database theory states that the sequence of columns in a table has no significance. The only way that the database management system can get at the data is through the column name, so sequence of columns is unimportant.

Exercise 3.16

To move a column, Click on the **column title bar** to select the whole column, which will go black to indicate the selection. Make sure the mouse cursor is on the title bar then click and drag the column to the right or the left until the desired column position is reached, then release the mouse button. The whole column will be moved to the new position.

It is conventional (but not required) to put the Primary Key fields in the leftmost position in a table. Rearrange the tables so that this is the case.

caution!

Changing the ordering of the columns in a table has no effect on any applications, queries, reports or forms that you may use. In theory, relational databases do not make any use of the sequence of the columns in a table, only their names. In practice Access 97 does use the number of the column in a table for some purposes, but re-ordering the columns does not change this numbering. Take a look at the Design View after re-ordering the columns in a Datasheet view. The sequence in the Design View is unchanged.

3.17. Find and Replace

Once tables start to become large, it is necessary to use more sophisticated tools to manage the data held in them. Find and Replace are extremely valuable in helping you to maintain your data.

caution!

If you are used to using Word, you should find the way that these tools operate very familiar, but this also has a drawback, because there is a crucial difference. By default, Find and Replace operates only within the selected column, not across the whole table or the whole database. This can cause some confusion unless you are aware of it.

Exercise 3.17

To find text within a column:

step **1.** Open the table in **Datasheet View**.

step **2.** Click the title bar of the column that you wish to search. The column will go black to show it has been selected.

step **3.** Click on **Edit | Find** and type in the text that you wish to find. This could be a whole field that you wish to match or a word or even part of a word.

step **4.** If you want your text to match part of a field, select **Any Part of Field** in the **Match** box. The other options are 'Whole Field' which will only match your text against the whole field contents, or 'Start of Field', in which case your text will match only the start of the field.

5. You can search the whole of the column, or from the top to the bottom (Down) or vice versa (Up). This is important when you expect to find more than one row that matches your search text.

6. **Search only current field** is probably selected. If you really want to search all columns in this table, uncheck this selection.

7. Click on **Find First**. This will find the first row that matches your search text. You can then repeatedly use **Find Next** to step through all of the records in that match, in turn.

Replacing text works in the same way, except that you specify the search text and the text that should replace the search text. You can use **Replace All** if you want Access to go ahead and make all the changes without stopping. This is a quick efficient way to change a lot of data in your database.

caution!

This is also a good way to destroy a lot of data if you use it incorrectly. Access will help to avoid the worst by giving you a warning when you change data in this way, but until you are fully familiar with Replace, it is better to step through changes one at a time so you can fully appreciate what is happening.

The Search and Replace facility can be made a lot more powerful with the use of wildcards. A wildcard character is a special symbol that can stand for one or many characters. You can use a mixture of ordinary and wildcard characters in your search text. See below for a selection of wildcard characters and their usage:

Char	Use	Examples
?	Matches any single character	?ob matches Rob or Bob
*	Matches any number of characters	win* matches window, wink and winter
#	Matches any single numeric character	#1 matches 11, 21, 91 etc.

3.18. Checking Spelling of Text Fields

Access 97 provides some simple spell checking tools. These are able to find simple spelling errors in text fields, but, of course, they can't correct some of the rather unusual words that you would typically find in song lyrics. The tables shown in Figure 3.13 contain some spelling mistakes. To find them Click on **Tools | Spelling**. You will see a Spelling window that is identical with those provided in the other Office 97 applications. You should **Ignore** or **Change** each of the words that are found, depending on whether they are really mistakes, or simply unusual words.

3.19. Filtering Rows

A filter allows you to select which rows you wish to see within a table. It is very important to recognise that a filter does not change any of the data in a table; all the rows are still there, even though they may not be visible.

A filter is a good idea when you want to:

- Work with just a small number of rows in a big table, and you don't want to hunt through all the table for those rows. In a big table, you might easily miss a few.
- Look at the data in a table in a special way, based on the contents of one or more columns.

Exercise 3.19

You can set up a filter from the table Datasheet View. Open the table and click on the **data value** that you want to select for viewing. Right click the mouse. You will see a small window displaying at its top a list of filtering options. Click on **Filter By Selection**. The datasheet will be redisplayed, showing only the rows that have the same value as the one you first selected.

Apply a filter to the Tracks table so that only the tracks from Blonde on Blonde are displayed. The result should look like Figure 3.15

Track : Table

Number	Name	Duration	CDCatalogRef
1	Rainy Day Women Nos 12 & 23	4.58	CDCBS 22130
2	Pledging My Time	3.72	CDCBS 22130
3	Visions of Johanna	7.5	CDCBS 22130
4	One Of Us Must Know (Sooner Or Later)	4.92	CDCBS 22130
5	I Want You	3.11	CDCBS 22130
6	Stuck Inside Of Mobile With The Memphis Blues Again	7.07	CDCBS 22130
7	Leopard-Skin Pill Box Hat	3.85	CDCBS 22130
8	Just Like A Woman	4.68	CDCBS 22130
9	Most Likely You Go Your Way And I'll Go Mine	3.4	CDCBS 22130
10	Temporary Like Achilles	4.82	CDCBS 22130
11	Absolutely Sweetmarie	4.78	CDCBS 22130
12	4TH Time Around	4.46	CDCBS 22130
13	Obviously 5 Believers	3.52	CDCBS 22130
14	Sad Eyed Lady Of The Lowlands	10.75	CDCBS 22130
0		0	

Record: 1 of 14 (Filtered)

Figure 3.15 Example of applying a filter to the Tracks table.

You remover the filter in the same way. Click on a value in the column that has the filter. Right click the mouse and click on Remove Filter.

information

Filters can also be used with forms.

3.20. Printing Tables

It is possible to print tables, just as they appear in the Datasheet View. This is of limited value, but can be useful for checking batches of data as you add records. Much better printing facilities are available when you design a report and we will cover this in Chapter 6.

Exercise 3.20

step **1.** Click on **File | Page Setup** to select the size of paper that you wish to use and the margins. These can be adjusted in the same way as for any other document. Once you have set up the page correctly, click on **OK**.

step **2.** Click on **Print Preview** to see a visual representation of your table. This is useful, because when your tables become much larger, you can check the number of pages that will be printed before you start wasting paper. The number of pages is displayed at the bottom of the Print Preview window. You should also check that everything else is in order before you start printing. Click on **Close** on the **Print Preview** window when you are satisfied with how the table looks.

step **3.** To actually print the table, click on **File | Print**, making sure that the correct printer and printing options are selected. Click on **OK** to start printing.

3.21. Closing Exercises

These exercises are intended to test your understanding of the work you have done so far. None of them require any significantly new techniques, but they are slightly more challenging than the exercises you have seen so far. You should complete all of these exercises before moving on to the next chapter. Sample answers are provided.

Exercise 3.21a

You have a lot of classical CDs in your collection. For these CDs, you are interested in the Composer and the Conductor as well as the artist (orchestra). You would really like to record the same type of details for a Composer as you have for an artist, i.e. date of birth and some historical notes. For Conductor you don't really want the date of birth, but the ability to store some notes is still useful. Remember that you will not always want to record the name of the Conductor and the Composer for all CDs, this would not make much sense for a typical pop CD.

Change your database design to allow for these extra features. Don't forget to make the necessary additional relationships. Is there a quick way to create the new tables?

Answers: You will need two new tables, one for Conductor and one for Composer. You could create these tables from scratch using the same approach we used earlier in the chapter, but you may have noticed that they are both very similar to the Artist/Band table we started with. You can quickly create copies of a table by selecting the table in the Database View, then use Edit/Copy to put the table on the Clipboard. If you then do Edit I Paste you can choose to paste the new table as structure only, or with all its data. Clearly you only require the structure. You will also need to supply new names for the new tables. Once the new tables have been created, you should change them using the same approach we used in this chapter. You will delete the Date Of Birth from the Conductor table.

There is slight problem with the Date of Birth field for Composer, in that you probably don't know the full date of birth for many of them, just their birth year. For the present, you can get around this problem by entering the date as 1 January in the relevant year.

A Composer can compose the music on many CDs, but for our purposes we will assume that each CD has only one Composer. A Conductor can conduct different pieces of music on many different CDs, but we will assume that one CD features only one Conductor. Both of these assumptions are reasonable, but might occasionally be invalid for a few special cases.

Based on this analysis, both of these new tables have a one to many relationship with the CD table, so you need to add new fields to the CD table to represent the links to the new tables.

Once this is done you should use the relationship tool to make the relationships between the tables clear to Access.

Figure 3.16 shows the Design view for all three tables. Notice that we have not made Composer and Conductor in the CD table Required, because we don't want to have to provide this data for all CDs.

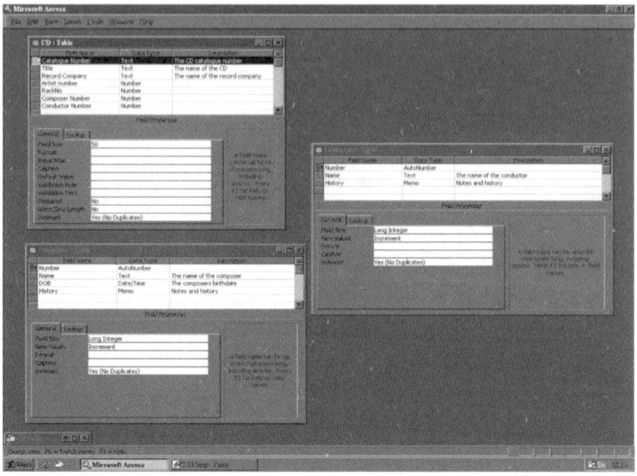

Figure 3.16 Design view for all three tables.

Figure 3.17 shows the relationships.

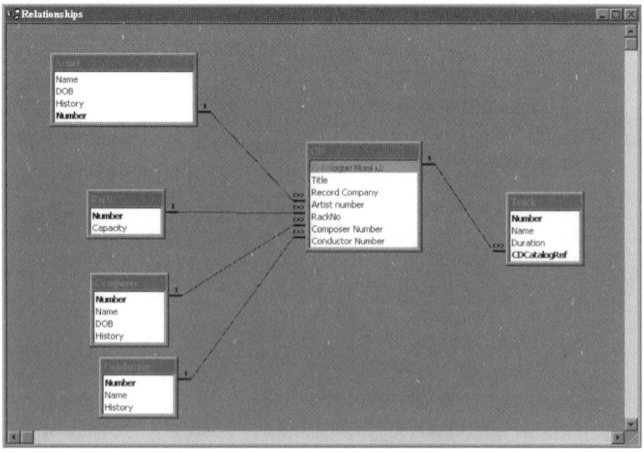

Figure 3.17 Making the relationships clear between the tables.

Exercise 3.21b

Add data for the following CDs: Notice that data is not provided for some of the fields.

Title :	Brandenburg Concertos 2 & 3
Record Company:	HMV
Catalogue Number:	HMV 7 67606 2
Artist Name:	Academy of St Martins in the Fields
Conductor:	Neville Marriner
Composer:	J.S. Bach
Date of Birth:	1685
Rack Number;	1, which can store 150 CDs

Tracks:

1	Brandenburg Concerto No 3	13.58
2	Concerto for Two Violins	16.92
3	Sheep May safely Graze	4.53
4	Jesu Joy of Man's Desiring	5.20
5	Suite No 3 in D	18.58
6	Brandenburg Concerto No 2	15.23

3.22. Summary

This long chapter has covered some of the most difficult aspects of developing a database. We have seen that you need to carry out an analysis of business requirements before starting to create tables, and that this analysis is the key to obtaining a useful, reliable database.

Access provides a good set of tools for setting up the tables that comprise your database, but you need to make full use of these, especially Primary Keys and relationships, to build an effective database.

All the remaining chapters in this guide build on what we have learnt in this chapter. It is important that you are fully confident before you proceed, so do not hesitate to revise the material before moving on.

4

Retrieving Information

In this chapter you will learn how to

- *Create a simple query.*
- *Find a record based on given criteria.*
- *Save a query.*
- *Create a query with multiple criteria.*
- *Select and sort data based on logical operations.*

We have now seen how we can design a database, implement that design in Access 97 and populate the tables with some data. Databases are much more than simply a container for storing data. In Chapter 1 we emphasised how the retrieval of data from a database in such a way that we can solve real world problems was an important goal. To achieve that goal we need to be able to query a database.

4.1. Queries

A query is a request to the database management system to retrieve some data.

In the previous chapter we put a lot of effort into getting a good design for our database. One of the reasons for that effort was so that we would be able to ask a range of questions about our data, some of which could be very complex, and obtain correct answers.

One of the fundamental ideas underlying the theory of relational databases is that all queries work on tables and every query produces a table. This is helpful, because we already know a lot about tables and how they behave.

It is useful to keep this model of a query in mind as we work through this chapter. A query can draw data from one, or more than one, table and combine it together to produce a result table, which Access calls a Dynaset. See Figure 4.1.

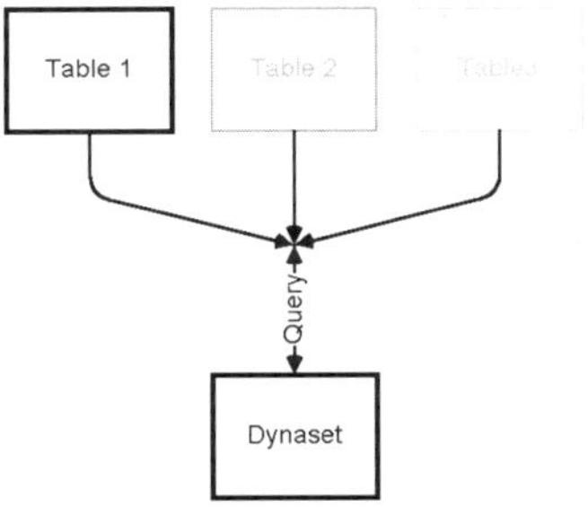

Figure 4.1 A query combining data to produce a Dynaset.

Queries are very important in making Access useful for real business applications. So far we have worked with data at the raw table level, but you would not want to work in that way all the time. We can design queries and then save the query.

information

We phrased the last sentence in a rather specific manner to emphasise an important point. When we save a query, we are saving the definition of the query, the question we are asking of the database. The result of running the query – the Dynaset – is not saved. This is re-generated every time we use the query, so the results are always up to date.

These queries can then be used to construct forms and reports, which are essential for real business applications. This chapter is therefore an essential building block for the last two chapters in the guide.

There are a variety of ways in which you can construct a query, but Access 97 uses a simple but powerful approach called Query By Example (QBE). This is easy to learn because instead of needing a new language to define a query, you essentially show Access an example of the data that you want and QBE finds the data for you.

Queries are the second major part of Access 97 that we have investigated (the first being tables), so we will start in the same place with the Database Window. This has a tab for queries, just to the right of the Table tab. A query can be constructed starting from this tabbed window. Click on the **Query Tab** and then on the **New** button. This will open the New Query window, which should look like Figure 4.2

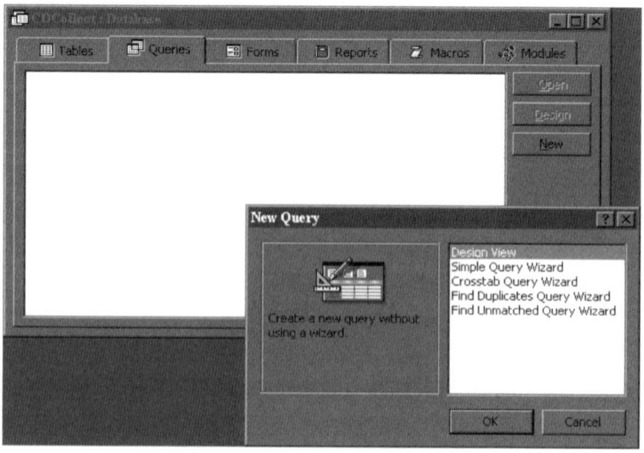

Figure 4.2 The New Query window.

- Design View is the main tool we will use for constructing queries.
- Simple Query Wizard provides a simple step-by-step Wizard based approach for building queries, but like all wizards, if you want to do something a little different this is not the tool to use.
- The Crosstab Query tool is used to construct a very specialised type of query that we will not consider in this guide.
- The Find Duplicates Query Wizard is a useful tool for defining queries that can find rows with duplicated values. We won't cover this tool, but you should remember that it is available and use it if you find it necessary.
- The Find Unmatched Query Wizard helps you build a query that can locate rows in one table that do not have related rows in another table. This is again a useful tool, but not one you will need to use for constructing simple database.

information

You may be wondering if all database management systems provide the same types of queries in the same way as Access. It is difficult to answer this in a simple way. Database management systems intended for small databases, as opposed to enterprise scale databases tend to use a variety of methods to define queries. Large scale Relational Database Management Systems all use a special language to define queries called the Structured Query Language (SQL). This allows very sophisticated queries to be created, but a fair amount of training is needed to use this properly. Access also allows queries to be created using SQL, but we will not consider this in the guide.

We will start by considering queries based on a single table. These are much simpler to construct and this will help us to describe the different tools that we can use. We will return to queries that take in more than one table later.

4.2. Using the Query Wizard

The Query Wizard is a good starting point for simple queries.

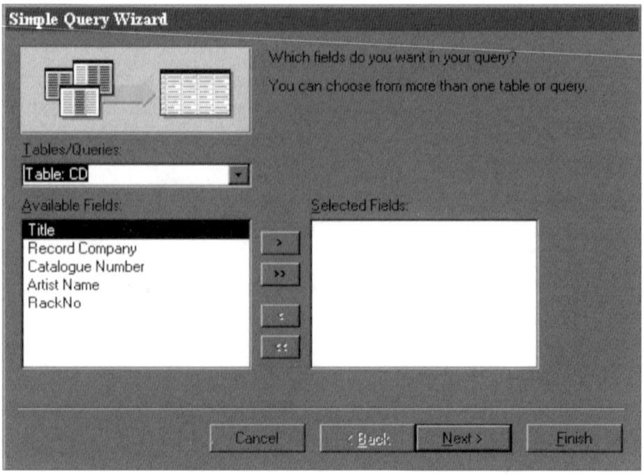

Figure 4.3 First stage of the Query Wizard.

The first stage of the wizard (see Figure 4.3) prompts you for the fields that you will use in your query. Select the table in which the fields can be found. The wizard will then display the names of the fields in the Available Fields window.

Select the fields you need by double clicking on their names, or clicking the right arrow button. The field name will then appear in the right hand side window.

If you need all the fields, click on the double right arrow button. If you make a mistake and select the wrong field, use the left arrow button to put it back into the Available Fields window. If you want to put all the fields back, use the double left arrow.

The next section of the wizard will ask you to name the query. You can use any name you like, but it is useful to follow a consistent naming scheme so that you can quickly recognise a particular query.

The wizard will ask you if you wish to open the query to view information or to modify it. These two options correspond to the table datasheet and table design views we used in the last chapter. The same facilities are presented for queries.

Just as we saw for table design, the wizards are useful but we also need to understand how to construct a query using the Design View.

4.3. Creating a Simple Query

Before we started to implement our CD database in Access 97, we first spent some time designing the database on paper. This is also a good strategy for designing queries. A little time thinking about what you need can save a lot of work.

When you design a query, you can specify the following:

1. The tables from which data will be extracted. For a simple query we will work with only one table.

2. The fields within these tables that will be involved in the query.

3. The specific rows that you require. You can limit the result to rows that meet a particular criteria.

4. The order in which rows should appear in the result.

5. Calculations based on data in the tables you specify.

We will use our CD database as the basis for exploring queries. An obvious query would be one that found all the tracks for a particular CD, putting them in sequence. Using the numbered analysis above:

1. The table required is Track;

2. We want to see data from the Number, Name and Duration fields of the table;

3. We will want to select rows based on the CDCatalogRef field;

4. The result should be put in order of the Number field.

Now we can implement this query using Access.

Exercise 4.1

Start from the CDCollect Database window. Click on the **Query** tab. You should see one query already in the window, this is the one you created earlier with the Wizard. Click on **New** and this time select **Design View**. See Figure 4.4.

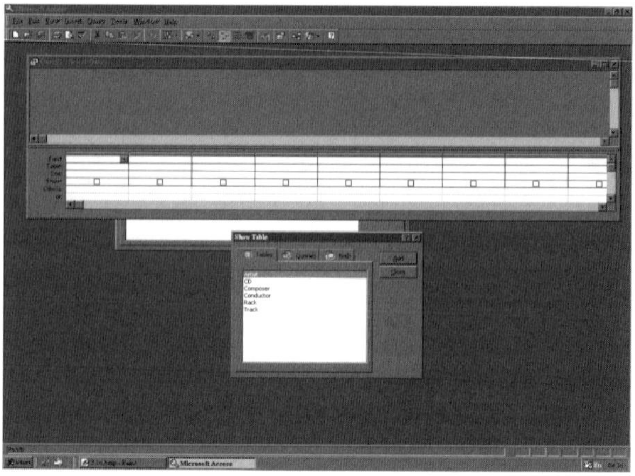

Figure 4.4 The Design View window used for selecting tables.

The **Show Table** window allows you to select the tables that will be used in this query. We only want the **Track** table, so select this and click on **Add**, then click on **Close** to remove the Show Table window. You can always add further tables if you want to change a query later.

information

You may have noticed that Show Table has three tabs, Table, Queries and Both. This is because you can use both tables and queries to build new queries. Remember that a query produces a Dynaset, and this can be used like any other table in a query. We don't need to use this capability at the moment.

Now we need to select the Fields that we will use in the query. The available fields are displayed in the upper part of the Query window, shown in much the same way as in the Table Design view. The bottom part of the window is the working area in which you assemble these fields to create your query. This area consists of a number of columns, each of which can contain a Field. Double click on the required field in the upper part of the Window. Access will display this field in the next available column. Carry on doing this until you have all the relevant Fields in the bottom part of the window shortcut

If you prefer, you can drag the fields from the top part of the window to the lower, working area.

You can change the sequence of the fields. Click on the bar at the top of the column and then drag the column to the left or the right. You can delete a column from the query working area by clicking on the top bar then pressing the Delete or Del button on the keyboard.

We don't really want to see the CDCatalogRef on each row of the Dynaset, so 'untick' the **Show** box in this column.

We want the Dynaset sorted in ascending order based on the value of the Number field. Click in the **Sort** row of the **Number** column and select **Ascending**.

We need to test our query, so we will ask Access to extract only those tracks that belong to the Catalogue Number *CDCBS 22130*. Type this in the Criteria box for CDCatalogRef. Notice that Windows puts double quotes around this input for you. At the end of this, your query should resemble Figure 4.5

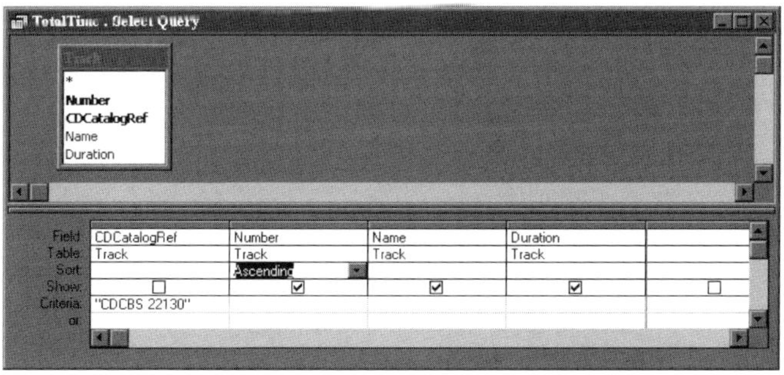

Figure 4.5 Your query should look like this.

Close the window, and when prompted give the query a suitable name. You can also save the query by using the **File | Save** and **File | Save As** menus. The **Save As** option allows you to save an edited query under a different name.

You can now test the query by selecting it in the CDcollect Database window and then clicking **Open**. This will force Access to run the query and present the results to you, which should look like Figure 4.6

TotalTime : Select Query

Number	Name	Duration
1	Rainy Day Women Nos 12 & 23	4.58
2	Pledging My Time	3.72
3	Visions of Johanna	7.5
4	One Of Us Must Know (Sooner Or Later)	4.92
5	I Want you	3.11
6	Stuck Inside Of Mobile With The Memphis Blues Again	7.07
7	Leopard-Skin Pill Box Hat	3.85
8	Just Like A Woman	4.68
9	Most Likely you Go your Way And I'll Go Mine	3.4
10	Temporary Like Achilles	4.82
11	Absolutely Sweetmarie	4.78
12	4TH Time Around	4.46
13	Obviously 5 Believers	3.52
14	Sad Eyed Lady Of The Lowlands	10.75
0		0

Record: 1 of 14

Figure 4.6 Presentation of query results.

The result of running the query is a Dynaset, and as you can see, it looks just like a table.

Now you know how to construct a simple query, everything else we will cover in this chapter can be tackled in easy stages, building on this foundation.

4.4. Specifying Criteria and Using Expressions

First we need to be able to select rows rather more flexibly than just typing in the whole of a value such as CDCBS 22130. This would quickly get tedious, and certainly doesn't help when you want to select rows according to a comparison with another value, a technique that you will find especially valuable.

To understand criteria better we need to be able to put together 'expressions'. These vary according to the type of data that you have stored in a field.

information

You may find it useful to revise section 3.16, where we discussed wildcards. Expressions use some of the same features.

We will start with the simple wildcards:

Char	Use	Examples
?	Matches any single character	?ob matches Rob or Bob
		he?? Matches help, head and heat
*	Matches any number of characters	win* matches window, wink and winter
		ar matches March, garden and embargo
#	Matches any single numeric character	#1 matches 11, 21, 91 etc.

We can do comparisons:

Character	Meaning	Examples
<	Less than	< 1024 matches rows with values less than 1024
>	Greater than	>5 matches numbers greater than 5
		>Bill matches all words that are alphabetically higher, e.g. car, door, elephant etc.
>=	Greater than or equal to	>= 10 matches 10 and all higher numbers
<=	Less than or equal to	See above
Between...And	A range of values	Between 12/10/95 and 12/12/99 matches all dates between these dates

Notice that you can use these comparisons with dates, numbers and text. Mixing different type of data does not usually make sense, so if you have a date field, comparing it to "California" would not be useful. We can connect bits of expressions together to make more complex expressions. To achieve this we use a form of English based on a few key words.

Word	Meaning	Examples
Or	Either Value	Bill or John matches any row that has the value Bill or the value John
And	Both values	>= 1/3/99 and <=1/12/99 will select all the dates that are later than 1 March 1999 and earlier than 1 December 1999
Not	Opposite to	Not B* would select only those rows that do not contain a word beginning with B.

information

Query Designer provides a lot more functionality in putting together criteria than we can cover in this guide, but you can achieve a great deal using just the tools we have described. This is one area where Access Help is an essential source. Look for "Design or modify a query" in Help topics and "criteria" and "Using wildcard characters in string comparisons" in Help Index for more information and starting points for more advanced techniques.

Exercise 4.2

Modify the TotalTime query so that it selects only tracks 2-6 inclusive, does not include the names of the tracks, but does show the catalogue number. Make the catalogue number the first column. Call this query MiddleTracks. Test the query by Opening the Dynaset.

The query should look like Figure 4.7 and the Dynaset Figure 4.8.

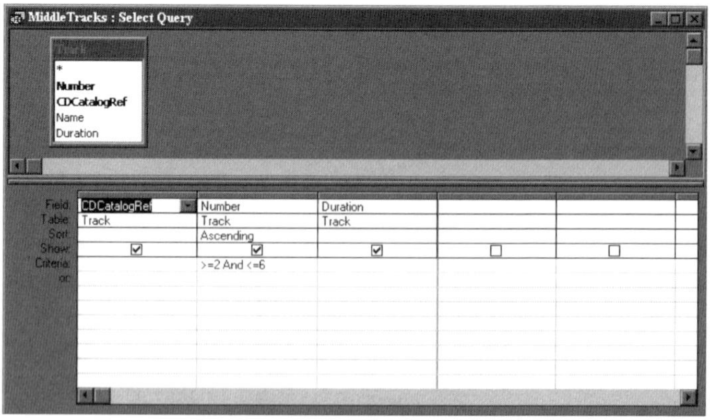

Figure 4.7 Your MiddleTracks query should look like this.

ECDL

MiddleTracks : Select Query

CDCatalogRef	Number	Duration
CDCBS 22130	2	3.72
COL 4678422	2	4.3
HMV 7 67606 2	2	16.92
CDCBS 22130	3	7.5
COL 4678422	3	4.6
HMV 7 67606 2	3	4.53
CDCBS 22130	4	4.92
COL 4678422	4	7.9
HMV 7 67606 2	4	5.2
CDCBS 22130	5	3.11
COL 4678422	5	2.9
HMV 7 67606 2	5	18.58
CDCBS 22130	6	7.07
COL 4678422	6	4.32
HMV 7 67606 2	6	15.23
*	0	0

Figure 4.8 Dynaset resulting from MiddleTracks query.

4.5. The Query Design Toolbar

Now we have seen the basics of designing a query we can begin to make use of some of the features that Access provides to make life easy. One of the most important of these is the Query Design toolbar. This, like the other Access toolbars is displayed automatically when you are carrying out query design activities. If it is not visible, you can display it by clicking on **View | Toolbars**. An annotated view of the toolbar is shown in Figure 4.9

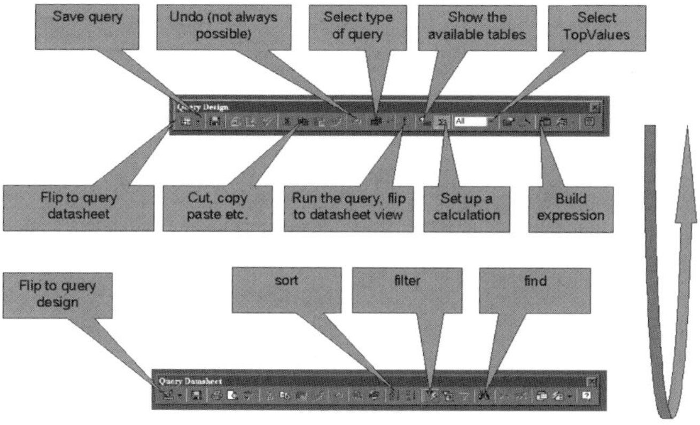

Figure 4.9 The Query Design toolbar.

We will not use all of these buttons in this guide, but see below for a short description of their functions, where these are not obvious, such as save, cut, paste etc.

- Undo: may allow you to undo the last change made to a query.
- Select type of query: helps to select the type of query you are building, this could be a Select query, a crosstab etc.
- Run: causes Access to run the query you have designed and display the result as a datasheet. It flips the toolbar to the query datasheet toolbar, which is shown below.
- Show the available tables: displays the window containing the names of tables.
- Put a Total row in the Query Design view: allowing the specification of a calculation.
- Select TopValues: is useful where a query could return a vast number of rows. It allows you specify that you want only the top 10 rows (for example) from the Dynaset. We will not cover this feature in detail.
- Build Expression: opens a window that helps you to build an expression easily.

4.6. Adding Calculations to Queries

Queries can perform calculations on the data in tables.

information

In Chapter 3 we warned against including derived or calculated data in your database tables. By using a query that contains a calculation we can obtain that calculated data without having to store it permanently. This is a good technique because you can be sure that the result of the calculation always reflects the current values of data in the tables.

A typical example of a calculation is where we require the sum or perhaps the average of a selection of rows grouped according the value of one of the fields. For example, we might want to obtain the total duration of all the tracks for our CDs, grouped or collected by the CD catalogue number.

This is easy to achieve with the Query Design window.

Exercise 4.3

1. Starting from the CDCollect database window, click on **New** and **Design View**.

2. Select the **Track** table and the two fields we require, CDCatalogRef and Duration.

3. Click on the Σ button. This will introduce a new **Total** row to the Query Design view.

4. Select **Group By** for the CDCatalogRef field, so that the totals will be grouped by the CD catalogue number.

5. Select **Sum** for the **Duration** field.

The resulting query should look like Figure 4.10

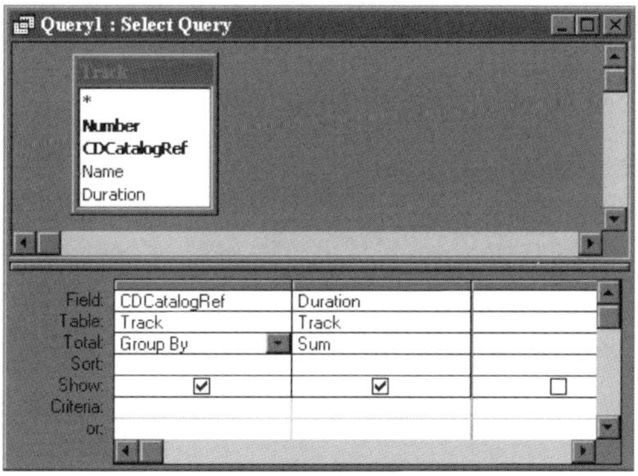

Figure 4.10 Example of query for total duration of all CD tracks.

Save the query as *CalcTotal*, then click on the **Run** button to test it. The Dynaset should look like Figure 4.11

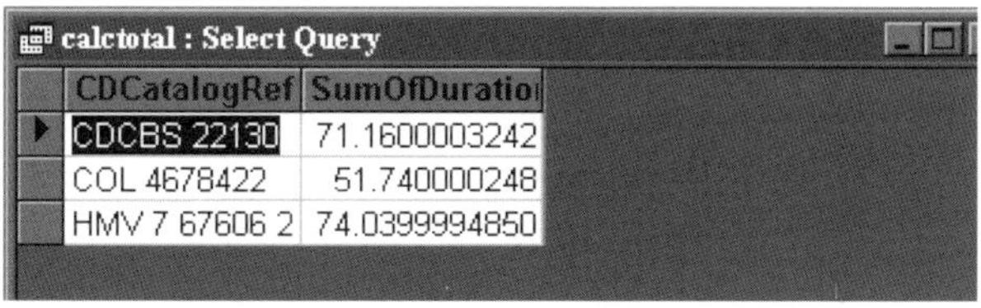

Figure 4.11 Dynaset resulting from CalcTotal query.

Modify CalcTotal so that it calculates the average track length per CD rather than the total playing time.

4.7. Adding a Filter

Filters can be used with queries in just the same way as for tables. Review section 3.18 for details of how we used filters in that context.

Exercise 4.4

To see how this works, return to the TotalTime query and open it with the **Query Design** view. Remove the criteria from the CDCatalogRef, so that all the rows will be selected.

Run the query to display the Dynaset.

If you click on the first row, which has a track number of 1, then click the **Filter by Selection** button, the Dynaset will be filtered so that only those rows with track numbers equal to 1 will be displayed.

caution!

The filter is not saved with the Dynaset, so if you run the query again, all the rows will be displayed. This may not be what you expected, but it is consistent with the dynamic nature of the Dynaset.

4.8. Queries Based on More than One Table

Whilst queries based on one table are useful, it is vital that you can construct simple queries based on more than one table, since these are the basis for much of the work that you will do with the forms and reports that we will cover in Chapters 5 and 6.

Queries can be based on two, three, four or even more tables, but the vast majority of multiple table queries will use just two tables and this is the type we will investigate. As well as the number of tables, the way we put the tables together in the query can vary a great deal, and this can become very complex. We will only use the simplest way of joining tables in a query.

caution!

You should gain experience with these simple two table queries before trying anything more adventurous. When you feel you are ready to try more complex queries, you should first do some general reading on relational database theory. A good general database textbook is Fundamentals of Database Systems by Elmasri and Navathe, published by Benjamin Cummings.

In Chapter 3 we showed how you could set up a relationship between two tables. We will base our two table queries on those relationships. An example will help to illustrate this idea. We need a query that will display the title of a CD alongside its total playing time. So using the same step by step approach as before:

Exercise 4.5

step **1.** The tables we need are Track and CD;

step **2.** We want to see data from the CD:Name and Track:Duration fields;

step **3.** We will want to select rows based on CDCatalogRef, which is shared between the two tables;

step **4.** The result should be put in order of the CDCatalogRef field.

Use the **Query Design View** to create a new query. Select the required tables from the **Show** table.

Notice that the two tables are shown in the same way as the Relationship window, with the connection between Catalogue Number in CD and CDCatalogRef in Track.

Add the required fields to the lower part of the window. These fields are **Title** from the CD table and **Duration** from the Track table.

Use the Σ button from the tool bar to open up the **Total** row, then add **Sum** to duration and **Group By** to Title.

The query should look like Figure 4.12

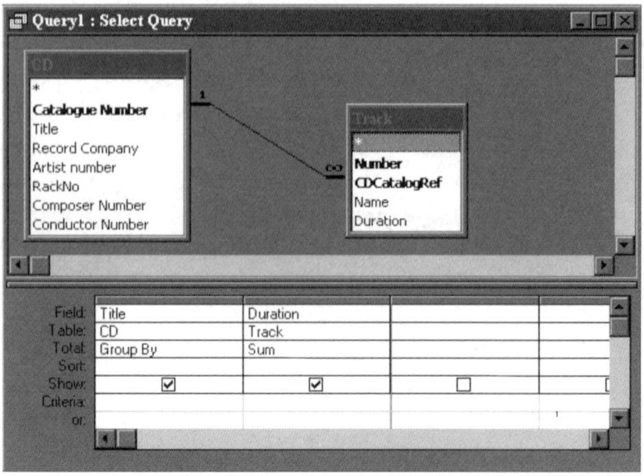

Figure 4.12 Example of a two table query.

Save the query as *JoinTable* and run it. You should see a result similar to Figure 4.13

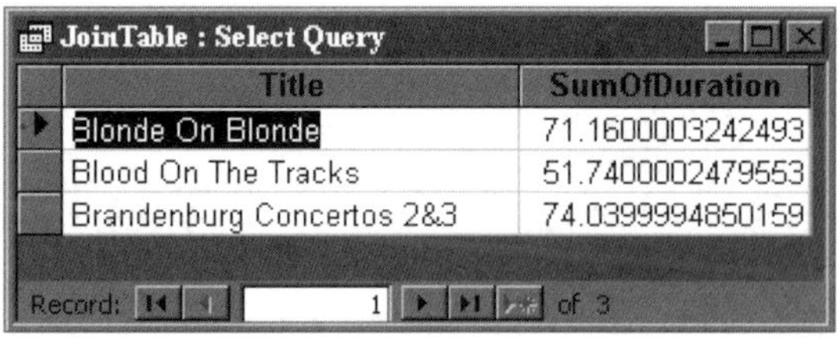

Figure 4.13 Result of the JoinTable query.

Do you think it matters that the sums column is displaying so many decimal places?

4.9. Summary

In this chapter we have seen how you can create a query based on the tables that form the core of your database. Queries play a central role in extracting data from those tables in a flexible way, and can also carry out simple calculations on numeric and date data. In the last two chapters of the guide we will apply what we have learned to derive screen-based forms and printed reports.

5

Using Forms

In this chapter you will learn how to

- *Use the Access Form Wizard to create a simple form.*
- *Create a form using the standard Access tools.*
- *Save a form.*
- *Arrange objects in a form.*
- *Use a query as the basis for a form.*
- *Enter data using a form.*
- *Format form text.*
- *Change the background colours and appearance of a form.*
- *Use graphics in a form.*
- *Print a form.*

Forms are an important, often indispensable part of many databases. Access provides tools that can be used to create extremely versatile forms and you will find working with these tools both easy and creative.

5.1. Why Forms are Useful

Paper forms are a part of everyone's working lives. We are used to filling in forms for such activities as tax, insurance, orders for products and services and general enquiries. Such paper forms are usually (eventually) typed into computer systems by data-entry staff.

A much better approach is to do away with the paper and to enter the data directly onto a form displayed by the computer. This has the following big advantages:

- The screen form can be made to look similar to an existing paper form, making it easy for people to switch from paper to computer use.
- The computer-based form can check what is entered as it is entered, so that only accurate data is processed.
- Using computer-based forms to replace paper preserves resources (trees) and saves on storage costs.

5.2. Basic Forms Ideas

In order to understand how forms work, we first need to recognise some basic ideas.

A form is built from a number of different components.

- Controls are areas where data can be entered or displayed by the computer. Some controls can be 'bound' to fields in the database. This means that they automatically display the value of the underlying database field, and if the data is changed in the control, it is changed in the underlying database.

Some examples of the limited selection of controls that we will cover in this guide are:

- Text Boxes – a control that displays text.
- Command Button – a control that issues a command to the database.

- List Box – a control that displays a list of things and allows the user to select one of them.
- Labels are textual descriptions that can be used anywhere within a form, but are often attached to a specific control, to inform the user what should be entered in that control.
- Graphics that can be as simple as lines and boxes, or as sophisticated as full colour pictures.
- Form Formatting Features such as headings and page breaks that can be used to give a form a recognisable structure. These are very important for forms that fill more than one screen.

Figure 5.1 illustrates many of these form features. This form is part of the Northwind sample database. You can investigate the design of this form at any time to see how the various effects have been achieved.

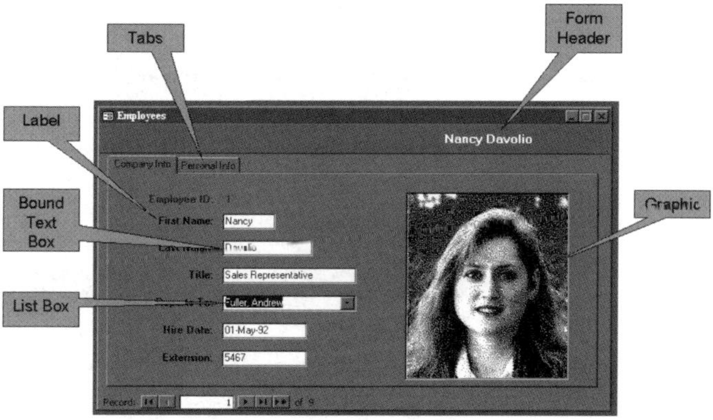

Figure 5.1 Example of a mix of form features.

5.3. Types of Access Forms

Access supports four different types of forms. These are described below, together with some examples taken from the Northwind sample database.

- A Single Column Form displays all the fields in a single column, with each field on a single line. This is about as simple as form layout can get, but it is quite acceptable for many purposes.

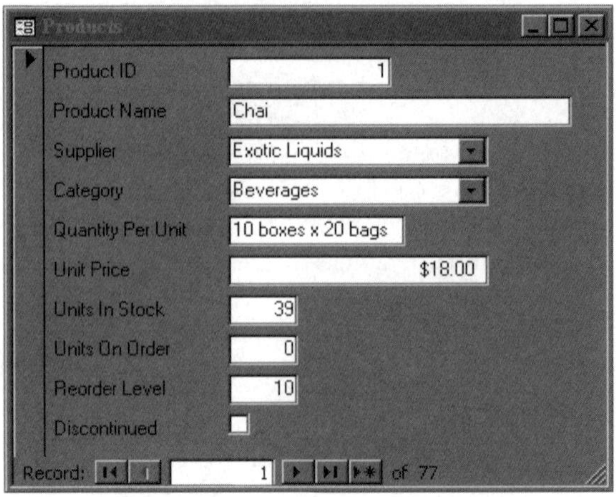

Figure 5.2 Example of a Single Column form.

- A Tabular Form is really just a form representation of the familiar Datasheet view that we used in Chapter 3. Each row in the table or query appears as a row in the table. The table column titles are used as column titles in the form. This type of form, like the single column is easy to set up.

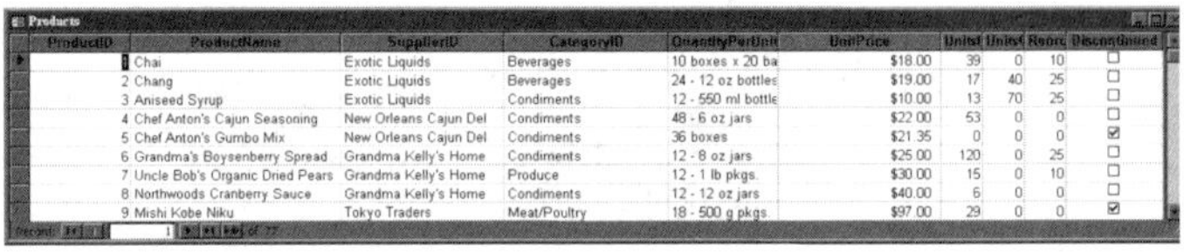

Figure 5.3 Example of a Tabular Form.

- A Main/Subform Form is designed to make it easy to represent the one to many relationship between two tables. Since this type of relationship is extremely common, a main/subform is used for a lot of different forms. This type of form requires a significantly greater effort to design.

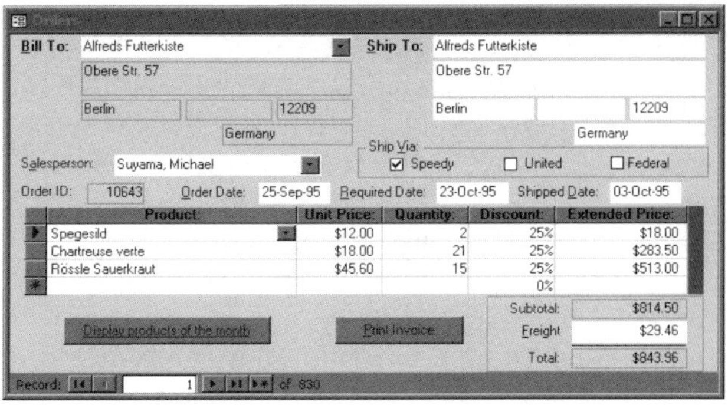

Figure 5.4 Example of a Main/Subform Form.

- A Graph Form displays data as a graph. There are a wide variety of these and if you have used Microsoft Excel you may be familiar with the range of charts. Popular choices are bar and line graphs.

5.4. Designing a Form

There is some benefit in doing some analysis of your forms before you start to work with Access. Think about the following points:

1. What process is the form meant to support? Don't try to design a do-everything form. This will usually be very hard for other people to use. Try to divide up the use of your database into two or three significant tasks that will need to be carried out, perhaps by different people. Each of these might need a form.

2. Who will use the form? If the typical user is a computer expert, you may be wasting your efforts producing a form that has a lot of visual frills. In contrast, if the typical user normally works with a paper form, then it is probably sensible to put a lot of effort into making your Access form look similar.

3. How often will the form be used? If data entry is needed only once a year or perhaps once a month, then it may not be necessary to design a form at all. As we saw in Chapter 3, simple data entry can be done directly into a table. If a form is used frequently, and by a large number of people, then it is probably necessary.

Given the previous thoughts, start your analysis of a new form by writing down the following:

1. The names or roles of the people who will be using the form.

2. The name of the process that the form will support.

3. The tables and fields that will be involved.

4. The way in which these fields will be used, for display only or for input.

Now draw out the form roughly on a piece of paper. Put the fields in a logical sequence and sketch in any graphical aids.

information

A form can be bigger than a single screen. If you do design a large form, Access will display scroll bars so you can move around it.

caution!

Although it is possible to build big forms this is usually a bad design.

5.5. Creating a Form with the Form Wizard and AutoForm

As we have seen earlier, Wizards are a simple way to create standardised components of a database. A similar facility is available for forms, but this is supplemented by Autoforms. This tool allows you to build a form based on a single table completely automatically. The forms created by Autoform or Form Wizard can be modified to meet your needs, so this is a convenient starting point for your requirements. We will review both of these facilities.

Exercise 5.1

Start with the CDCollect Database window, and click on the **Forms** tab. Now click on **New**. This will display the various ways in which you can create a new form. Figure 5.5 shows the window and we describe the options below.

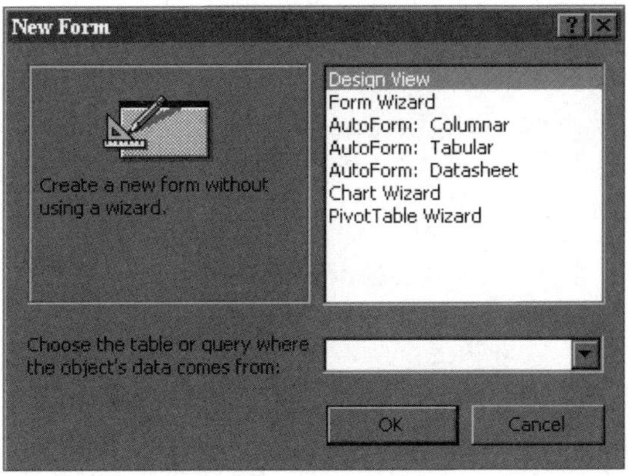

Figure 5.5 Options for creating a new form.

- Design View is the standard tool view, allowing you to build a form from scratch, or to modify an existing form.
- Form Wizard takes you through form design in a conversational manner.
- Autoforms are available for three different types of form.
- Chart Wizard helps you to build a graph as part of a form in a conversational process. We will not cover this tool in the guide.
- Pivot Table Wizard builds a form based on a pivot table. We did not cover pivot tables in Chapter 3. This type of form, whilst useful, is best ignored until more experience is gained with Access.

Select the **Form Wizard** and click the arrow in the drop down list. This will display a list of all the tables and queries we have defined in CDCollect. The Form Wizard can work with either queries or tables. Select **Artist** and click on the **OK** button.

Form Wizard will display a window asking which fields you wish to use in the form. This should be familiar from your work with queries. Select all the fields by clicking on the **right facing double arrow**, then click on **Next**.

Form Wizard will display a window asking which type of table you require. The choices are:

- Columnar;
- Tabular;
- Datasheet;
- Justified.

The first three should be familiar, but the fourth type is new. Click on the bullet and note how Access shows you a picture of a typical justified layout.

We will use **Justified** for this form, so select this and click on the **Next** button.

The next window asks what style you would like. These will be at least ten different styles available through this window. As with the form type, you can click on the bullet and see a depiction of the form. Try this for all the styles.

We will select **Standard**, so click on this choice and then click on the **Next** button.

The final window will ask for a form title. We will call our form *Artist*. Click on **Finish** to see the completed form, which should be as shown in Figure 5.6.

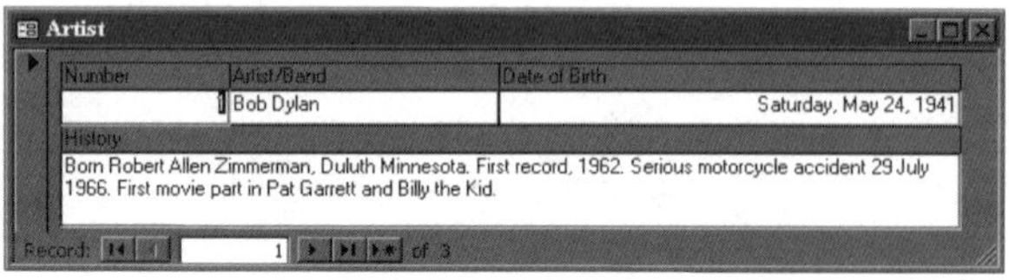

Figure 5.6 The completed form.

Using Autoform is even easier than the Wizard.

Exercise 5.2

Start from the CDCollect Database window. Click on **New**, then select **Autoform:Columnar** and the **Composer** table. Click on **OK** to create the table.

Since using Form Wizard and AutoForm is so easy, why do we need to use anything else?

If you need to produce a form that looks like a paper version, or you need to produce a form that is based on two or more tables, you will need to use the Form Design View.

5.6. Form Design Toolbar

Make sure that the Form Design Toolbar is displayed. Figure 5.7 shows the main features of the toolbar and the corresponding Form View toolbar.

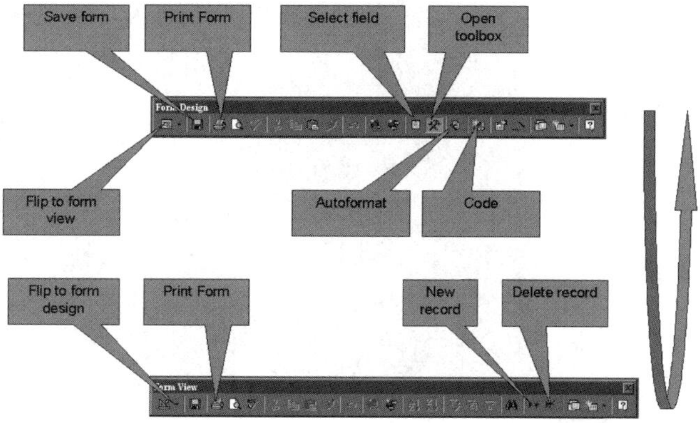

Figure 5.7 Main features of the Form Design toolbar.

Most of this will be familiar, but the following buttons are significant:

- Select Field: selects the fields that you can use in the form. Drag the required field to the correct position on the form.
- Open Toolbox: opens an additional toolbar containing icons useful for designing the form. Click on this icon if the toolbox is not visible.
- Autoformat: provides part of the functionality of the Form Wizard. It is useful for applying a consistent format to a series of forms.
- Code: is used for programming purposes. We will not cover any aspect of this significant, but complex component of Access.

5.7. Creating a Form using Design View

Exercise 5.2

Start from the CDCollect Database window. Click on **New** then select **Design View**. We will base our form around the **Track** table, so select this in the table box.

Access will display a blank form, with a grid layout, as shown in Figure 5.8. The grid is the pattern of dots and squares. If your form does not have a grid, click **View | Grid** to switch this on.

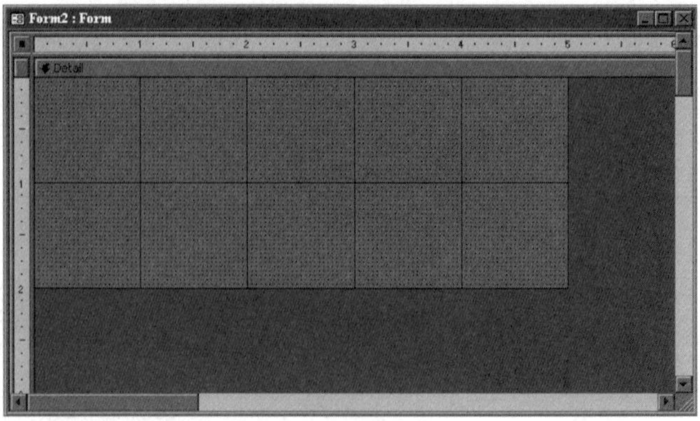

Figure 5.8 Blank form with grid layout.

The grid is very useful for rapidly lining up the different elements of a form. These will snap to the nearest grid point, making it easier to get a professional looking layout.

As well as a grid, your form should have a ruler. This is the measurement scale displayed along the top and left hand side of the window. The ruler can be used to place parts of your form at a precise measured position.

We will start by placing some text boxes on the form. These will be bound to the fields that belong to our selected table.

Click on the **Field List** button on the Form Design toolbar. This will display the field list. Now select **CDCatalogRef** and drag it onto the blank form. Place it at the bottom of the first row of squares. If you do not get it in the correct position on the first attempt, drag it into position.

Notice that we have actually placed two components. The right-most part is a text box, which is bound to the CDCatalogRef field. The left hand part is a label. You can change the size of the text box by dragging on the corners. The label will display the caption if one is defined for the field. When we designed the Track table, we did not supply a caption for this field, so Access uses the field name instead. This is obviously not ideal, but the label can be changed. We will change it to Catalogue Number. Figure 5.9 shows how it should look.

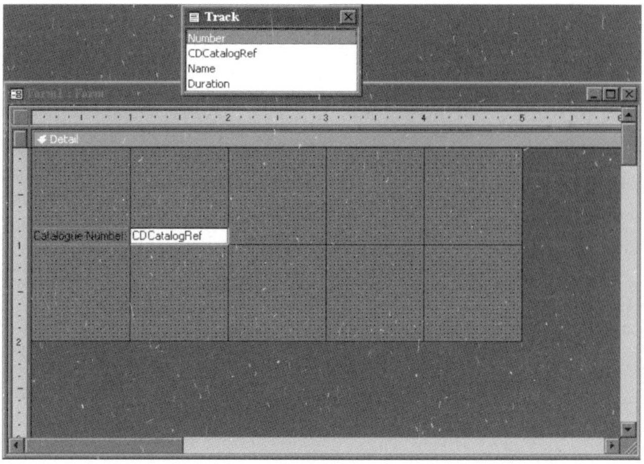

Figure 5.9 Label changed to Catalogue Number.

Add the other fields from the Track table to the form, keeping them lined up and providing better text labels where required.

The end result should be a layout such as Figure 5.10

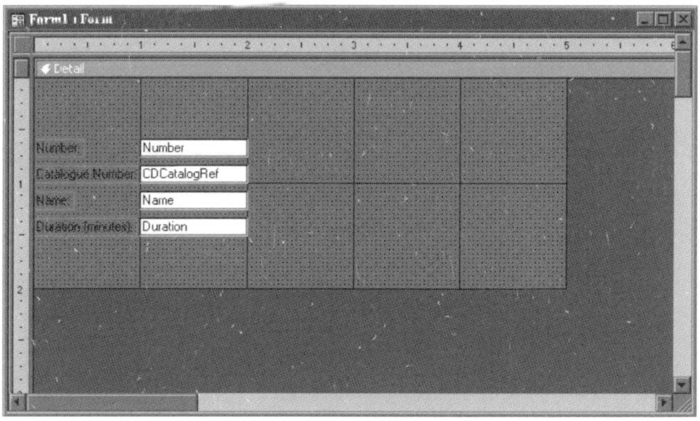

Figure 5.10 Your layout should look like this.

All the boxes are the same size in this design, but we need a much bigger box for the track name, so extend this box to the right so that we will be able to see a sensible amount of text.

Now we are ready to test our form. Display it by clicking on the **View** button on the toolbar. The result should look like Figure 5.11.

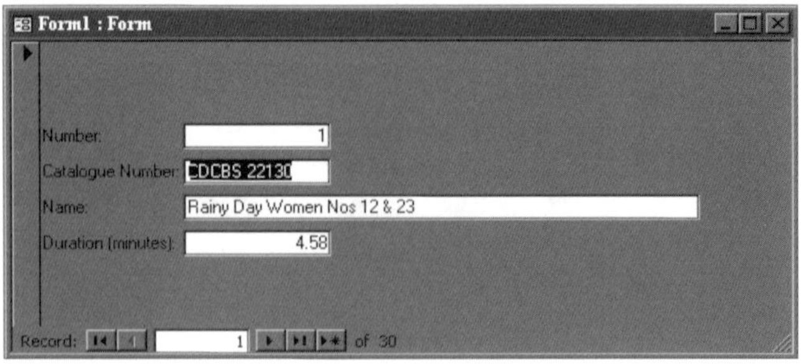

Figure 5.11 The result of the form creation using the View button.

Test the form by using the navigation buttons at the bottom of the window. The boxes displayed in the form are bound to the fields in the table, so you can modify the rows in the table by typing in new data. Test this by modifying the text of one of the track names.

The form works, but it doesn't look very professional. The boxes for Number and Duration are much too big, and we could really use a heading at the top of the form. Close the form and re-open it in **Design View** to make the modifications.

First modify the form to reduce the size of the relevant boxes.

To add a header to the form, right click in the grid area of the form. In the pop-up window, select **Form Header/Footer**. This will open new form areas at the top and bottom of the form as shown in Figure 5.12

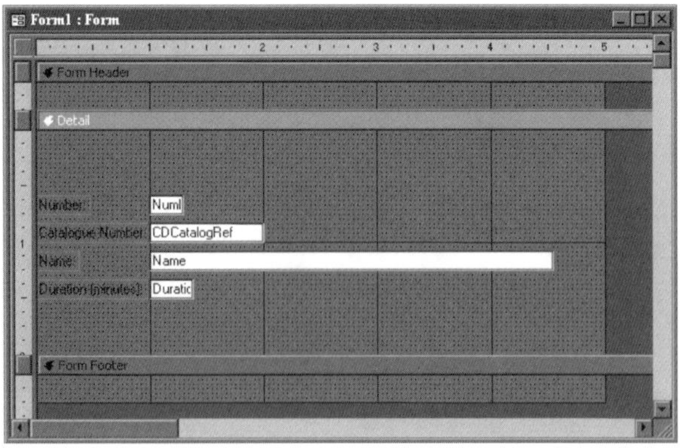

Figure 5.12 New form areas at the top and bottom of the form.

Now we will add a title in the header area. Ensure that the Toolbox is visible. Click on the **label** icon, then drag a rectangular area in the header. This will open up a text box.

This looks superficially like the text boxes that we can see in the Detail part of the form, but this box is unbound; it is not attached to any row in the database's tables. This means that it will not change as we look through the tracks.

Fill the box with some suitable text by typing in the box.

Check the results by clicking on the **View** button on the **Form Design** toolbar. The results will probably not inspire much enthusiasm. We need to increase the size of the text, perhaps use another font and some colour would be welcome. Go back to the **Design View** by clicking on the **View** button on the **Form Design** toolbar.

We need an extra toolbar to make our formatting efforts easier. Click on **View | toolbars** and select **Formatting (Form/Report)**. This will pop up a new toolbar as shown in Figure 5.13

Figure 5.13 Formatting toolbar.

We will not describe this toolbar in the same detail that we have used for the other toolbar, since it is so similar to the toolbars used for the other applications in the Office suite.

Select the **label** in the Header area and then pick a larger font size in the toolbar (about 20-24 points would be a good choice). While you are working with the text, try some different fonts.

Change the font colour using the **Font colour** button.

caution!

Make sure that you select the right hand side of this button so that you get access to the full set of available colours.

Now right click in the grid area of the header. Select an appropriate background colour from the menu.

Your finished form might look like Figure 5.14

Figure 5.14 Example of how your form might look.

shortcut

Don't forget that you can copy and paste a whole form from the database window. This is very useful if you need a series of forms that use a similar layout. Just make copies of the first form, then add and remove fields to get the desired results.

Exercise 5.3

Your form is now looking a little more acceptable, but it could be made even tidier. The number box shows the same data as the navigation bar at the bottom of the window, so the box is superfluous. Delete the Number box from the form design and re-arrange the rest of the form to suite. Save the form as TrackForm.

5.8. Adding Graphics to Forms

You can add graphics to a form by simply posting in a picture from another application. A good source of such graphics is the Office Clip Art Gallery. Click on **Insert | Object** and select **Microsoft Clip Art Gallery**. Choose your clip art and then click on **Insert**. You can move and resize the clip art graphic to achieve the desired effect.

5.9. Printing a Form

It is possible to print a form. This is often very useful, since a form can be used to retrieve data from one or more tables and the resulting information may need to be used away from the computer screen.

To print a form, make sure that the required data is displayed and then click on the **Print** button on the toolbar, click on **File | Print** on the main menu. Print preview is also available, if you would like to check how your form will appear before you print it.

caution!

If you find that you need to print out a lot of records, printing forms is a clumsy and time-consuming approach. It would be much better to design a report and let Access do most of the repetitive work for you.

5.10. Summary

Forms are easy to produce and the Wizards can help a great deal. We have seen how a form can be based on a table or a query and have produced forms that use different fonts, backgrounds and graphics.

6

Reporting

In this chapter you will learn how to

- *Use the Access Report Wizard to create a simple report.*
- *Sort data for presentation in a report.*
- *Modify reports.*
- *Use graphics in a report.*
- *Create and customise headers and footers.*
- *Group data in report totals and sub-totals.*
- *Use simple expressions in reports.*

All database packages provide tools to help you generate printed output from the database, and Access is no exception. In this final chapter, we will investigate the types of report that we can produce and the ways in which we can arrange information within them.

6.1. When to Use Reports

A report presents information drawn from a database. The key idea is that a report takes indigestible data (rows from tables) and turns it into information that is usable for a particular problem or requirement. We can present the same data in a host of different ways to suit different needs.

Some examples of reports are:

- Mailing labels ready to stick on envelopes.
- Mail merge letters using data drawn from a database.
- A summary, grouped into categories, with sub-totals for each category and a grand total for all categories. This is typical of management reports and accounts.
- A graph showing how data varies over time. Prices are often shown in this way.

You will typically use reports where you want to present information in a formal way, as a document that will be printed and perhaps bound. To meet this requirement you will need all the typical features of a document, including page layout, margins, headers, footers and page numbers. Access reports provide all of these features for you in an easy to use form.

Reports are similar to forms, and we construct them using some of the same types of tools, but they have a different primary objective. Forms are mainly intended for use through a computer screen, but reports are designed for printing. This does not mean that you cannot print forms (we saw how to do this in Chapter 5), or view reports on screen, but that is not their main objective.

6.2. Some Example Reports

To illustrate the typical uses of reports we will return to the Microsoft sample database, Northwind.mdb that we viewed earlier. Open the database and select **Reports** on the Database window. You will see at least thirteen different report displayed. We will view the first three only.

information

Note the top button on the right of the window. Instead of the Open button that we have seen for tables, queries and forms we see a Preview button. This is because when we view the report on screen, we are essentially previewing the printed report. This reinforces our view that reports are mainly intended for reading on paper.

Select the alphabetical list of products and click on **Preview**. You should see the first page of a multi-page report.

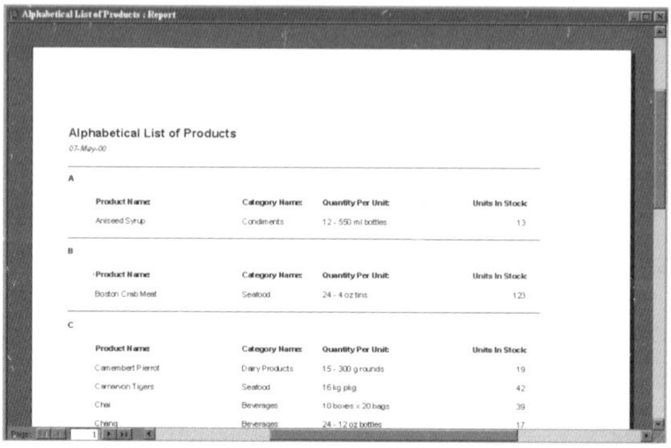

Figure 6.1 Viewing a report using Preview.

Page through the report using the video style controls at the bottom of the window. Now print the report using the printer icon in the Print Preview toolbar. Take a close look at the report. It uses heading and sub-headings and the output is grouped alphabetically. A sub total is provided for each alphabet letter. It is perhaps dubious whether a calculated total by alphabet is really useful, but it could just as easily be grouped by Category. Each page has a footer with a page number and the total number of pages. Access has calculated the number of pages before printing the report.

Close the Preview of the report and take a look at the Catalogue report in the same way. Don't waste paper printing this.

Figure 6.2 Viewing the Catalogue report using Preview.

Notice that this report has an entirely different style to the alphabetic listing. It is intended to be a selling document and has a particularly attractive appearance with full use of coloured graphics. The first two pages are fixed content, not drawn directly from the database tables. The main body of the report contains the same products that we saw earlier, but grouped by category. The final page is an order form, which again is fixed text. This type of presentation could not be produced using the forms that we encountered in the previous chapter. It is a perfect example of what you could achieve with your reports.

Finally we will review a third report. Close the Catalogue report and Preview the Customer Labels report.

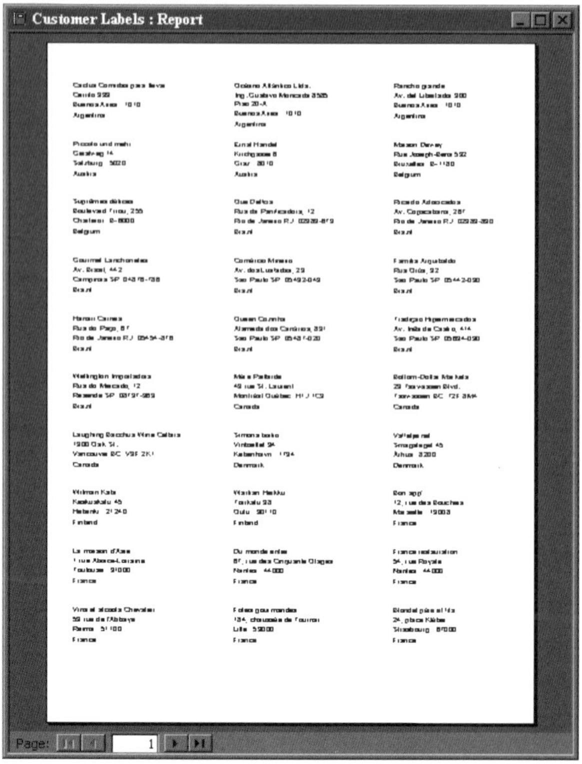

Figure 6.3 Viewing the Customer Labels report using Preview.

This looks far less impressive, but is just as useful. The report contains a list of all customer names and addresses laid out in rows and columns suitable for printing on sticky label stock. This would make it easy for Northwind to send a mail shot (perhaps the catalogue) to all its customers. This is a function that any mail order supplier would utilise.

6.3. Using the Report Wizard

As you have come to expect, Access provides a wizard that can produce a report layout with minimal effort. We will use the CD Collection database to try this out.

Exercise 6.1

Close the Northwind database and open **CDCollect.mdb** instead. Click on the **Reports** tab and then click on **New**. Access will present the familiar choices shown in Figure 6.4. Select the Report Wizard and the Track table.

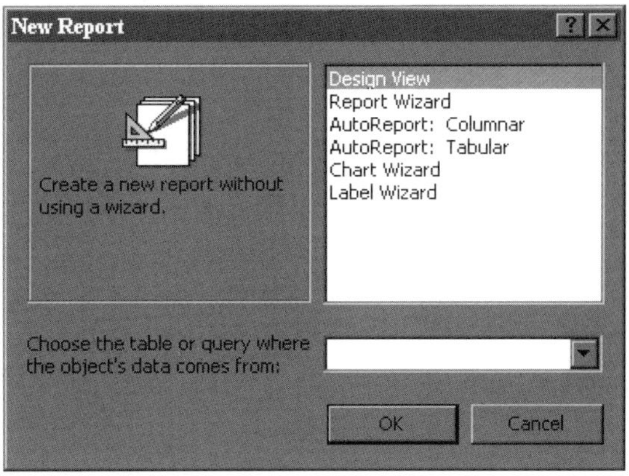

Figure 6.4 Selecting the appropriate report option.

The first stage of the Wizard follows exactly the same pattern that we saw for Queries and Forms. Select all the fields then click on **Next**. You should see a window resembling Figure 6.5

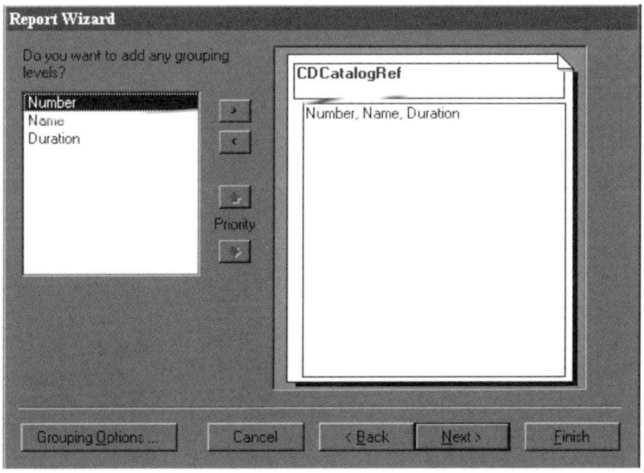

Figure 6.5 Selecting how to present report information.

This window is concerned with how your report will group information together. The picture in the right hand side of the window shows how the report will present the information. The Wizard has already decided that you will want to group information by CDCatalogRef, which is very sensible, but it is offering you the opportunity to change this and to select a sub-grouping if you need this. In this case, it would not make sense to group by any of the other fields so we will ignore this and continue to the next part of the Wizard.

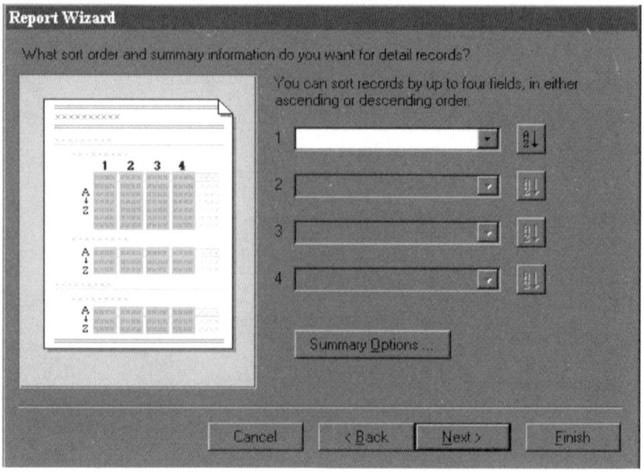

Figure 6.6 Deciding how information will be ordered.

The next Wizard section helps you to decide how the information in your report will be ordered and what sub-total you will use, as shown in Figure 6.6.

We would really like the tracks to be put in track number sequence, but no further ordering is necessary. If it was, we could select up three further levels of ordering. The report would sort the information on the first field, then sort the records that have the same value for that field using the second level field and so on. In most cases one or two level of sorting is plenty. The AZ icon adjacent to each field allows you to specify whether you would like the data sorted in ascending or descending order.

information

You have already used a similar type of facility in section 3.14. Revise that section for more information.

Click on the small arrow to drop down the list of fields for the first sort criteria and select **Number**.

We would like the Report Wizard to calculate the total playing time for the CD. To do this we must select **Duration** as our final sort criteria, but in this case click on the **Summary Options** and select **Sum** as the Summary Option. Click on **OK** to return to the Wizard.

information

Notice that you could also select other arithmetic functions at this stage, such as Average, Maximum and Minimum.

Click on **Continue** to move to the next stage of the Wizard, which is concerned with layout of data on the page. See Figure 6.7

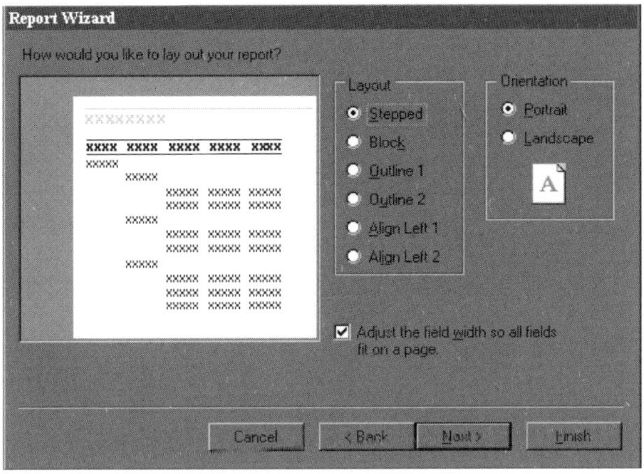

Figure 6.7 Deciding on the layout of data.

The diagram representing your final report is very helpful in understanding all the options. Try each of the **Layout** styles in turn, while observing the diagram. It is largely a matter of taste which of these style you select since each displays the same information, but in different places on the page. We will use the **Stepped** style for this example.

There is a small tick box which allows Access to adjust field width to make the information fit on the page. This is a sensible option for most reports, but you can always repeat the Wizard process if this does not give you the results you need.

The right hand side of the Wizard window contains the familiar paper orientation selections. Make your choice based on how you expect your report to be read. Most document-oriented reports will be portrait.

caution!

Access will use the default paper size for your copy of Microsoft Office. By default, this is often set to Letter size, which is mainly used in USA. You will probably want your reports to use the European paper sizes and in particular A4. If your reports don't fit the paper properly make sure you have the default paper size set correctly.

Click on **Next** to move to the next Wizard stage, which should look like Figure 6.8

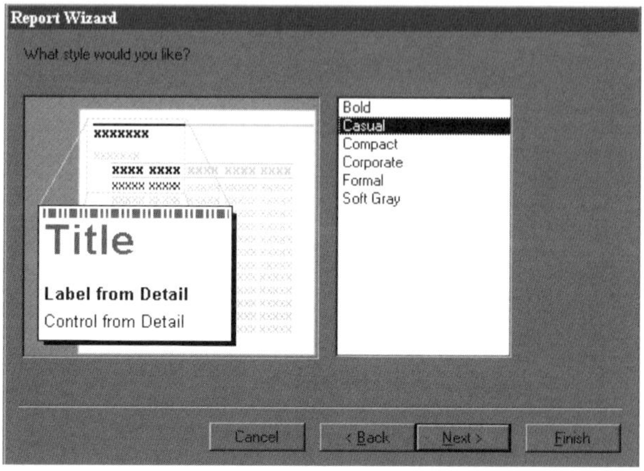

Figure 6.8 Selecting fonts, rulings and patterns.

As in the previous Wizard stage, we can select different styles for our report, but in this case it is the font and associated rulings and patterns that are made available. Try each of the bulleted options to find one that suits your needs. In this case, we are developing a report for personal use with a CD collection, so we don't want anything too formal. We will choose **Casual**. Click on **Next** to move on to the next stage of the Wizard.

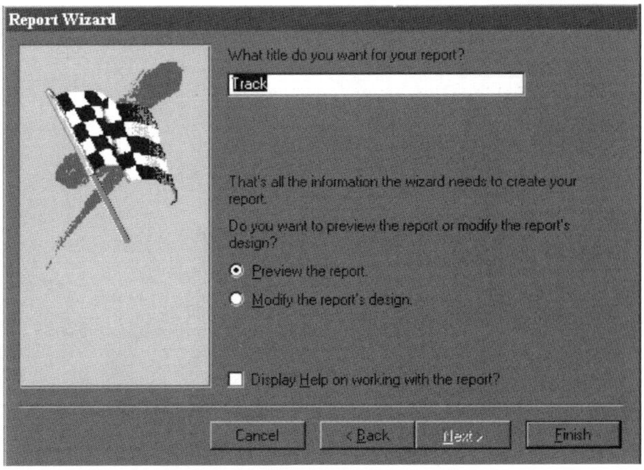

Figure 6.9 Selecting a title for the report.

The final stage of the Wizard allows you to select a title for the report and to preview or modify it. We will call the report *My CD Tracks*.

information

We have spent a little longer with the Report Wizard than with some of the other wizards that we encountered earlier. This is because it will probably be an appropriate tool to use for most of your reports. Where a minor variation is needed, it is easier to use the Report Wizard to produce a report and then modify it than to start from scratch. The exception to this would be a report that is highly stylised, such as the Northwind Catalogue that we saw earlier.

Click on **Finish** to see our report, which should look like Figure 6.10

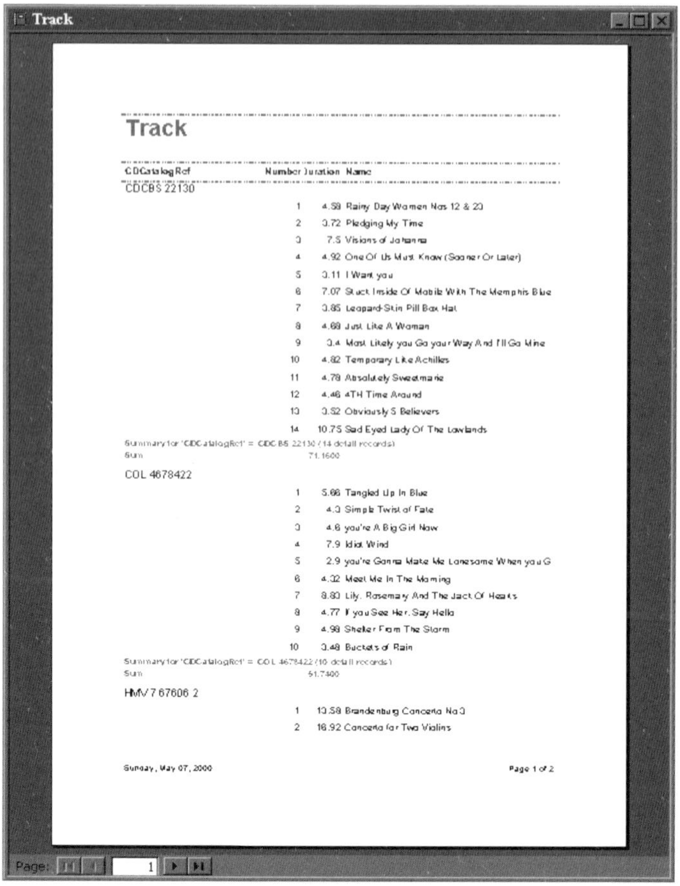

Figure 6.10 The final layout of the report.

The resulting report is not quite perfect. The Duration column needs a little more space and CDCatalogRef does not make a good column title.

One way to change the column title would be to edit the form, but we could achieve the same result in a different way that would probably be more useful. Can you think what this alternative is? If you are unsure, revise Section 3.11, particularly the **Caption** option.

6.4. Report Design Toolbar

The **Report Design** toolbar is similar in most respects to the Form Design toolbar we saw in the last chapter.

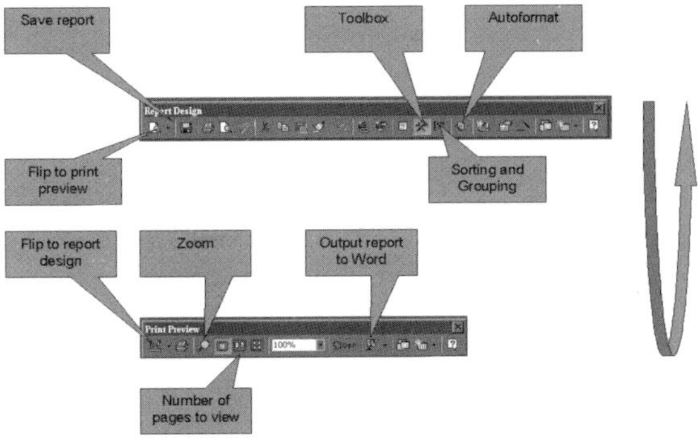

Figure 6.11 The Report Design toolbar.

As you would expect, the **Report Design** toolbar is twinned with the print preview toolbar. You can switch between them by using the buttons on the far left of each toolbar.

The zoom button is useful in checking report layout. The button toggles between two levels of magnification, making it easier to spot problems.

As with the Form Design toolbar, Autoformat allows you to use parts of the Report Wizard in your own reports. This can be very useful, avoiding a lot of detail work, but still giving you the freedom to design reports the way you want them.

The Output to Word button is actually more general than it might appear. You can use it to output forms to another Office application, rather than to a printer. The options include output to Word so that you can build a report into a word-processed document, or to Excel so that you analyse a database table as a spreadsheet.

6.5. Creating a Report Using Design View

Exercise 6.2

Start from the Database window, with the **Report** tab selected. Click on **New** to see the **New Report** window, as shown in Figure 6.12.

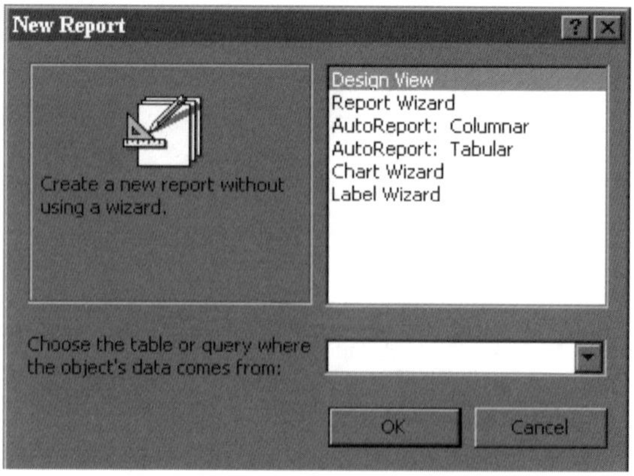

Figure 6.12 The New Report window.

We have already used the Report Wizard but there are five other options. The Design View allows you to build a report from scratch and we will explore this shortly. There are two AutoReport options, one for columnar and one for tabular layouts. We will not review these options, but you should investigate these when you have gained some familiarity with reports. They can be a big time saver in the same way as the Report Wizard.

The Chart Wizard is useful for preparing reports that contain a chart, such as a graph. This again is well worth investigating if you need to produce this type of report occasionally.

The Label Wizard is focussed on producing mailing lists. This is a very specialised wizard, but as we have seen, many people want to produce mailing labels so the Wizard is very helpful. We will not review this in detail.

information

If you plan to use this, you will find it helpful to decide on your label format (size and number per sheet) by selecting from the popular Avery label series. The Wizard uses the Avery label numbers so by choosing one of these, most of the work is done by the Wizard.

To use the Design View, select the table or query that you wish to use, then click on **OK**. We will use **Artist** for our example, arranging the report in a simple tabular fashion

An empty report will be displayed as shown in Figure 6.13

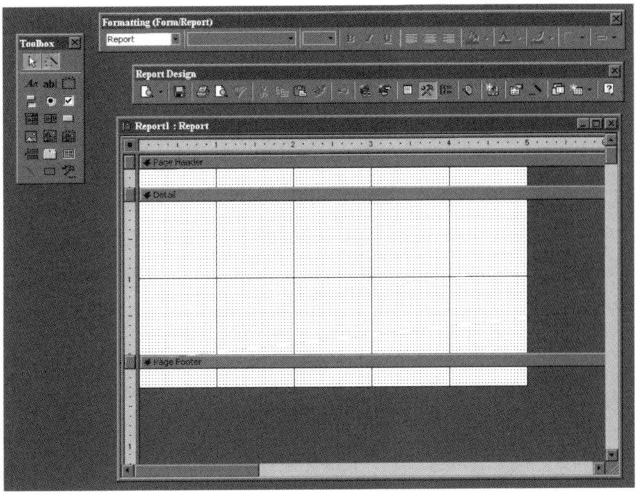

Figure 6.13 Empty report produced under Design View.

The report has three sections, just like the form. We will concentrate on the Detail section first, which will contain information about Artists, one row for each Artist. Click on the **Field List Button** to display the available fields from the Artist table. We will select only **Name**, **DOB** and **History** from the list. Click on each one in turn and drag them to the Detail section of the report. Line them up one on top each other to begin with, so the result will look like Figure 6.14

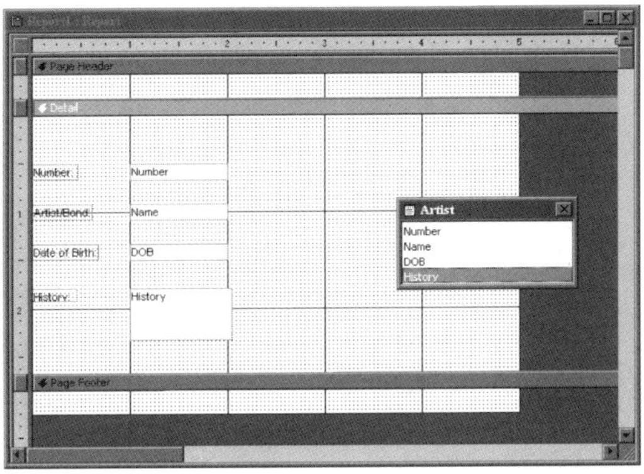

Figure 6.14 Selecting the report components.

The fields are all bound to the underlying database table, exactly as we require, but the labels are not where we want them. For a tabular layout, they should be at the top of each column, not immediately to the left of each field. We can fix this very easily. Drag through the labels, selecting only the labels and not the fields. Now select **Edit | Cut** from the main Access menu. The labels will disappear from the Detail section. Now click inside the **Page Header** area and use **Edit | Paste** from the main Access menu. The labels will be pasted into the header area, without disturbing the fields.

caution!

You might think that you could simply drag the labels to the header area. Unfortunately, this will not work. You must use the Edit | Cut and Edit | Paste routine.

Now line up the fields and labels so that they take up an appropriate amount of space and line up with each other. The History field could contain a lot of text, so give this plenty of page width. While you are working with the Page Header, add a suitable report title. We will assume that this report will be printed on a monochrome laser printer, so we don't need special colours.

Your Report design should look something like Figure 6.15.

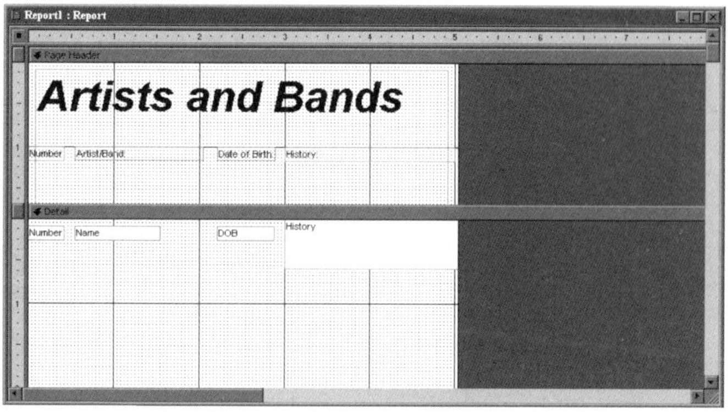

Figure 6.15 Example of how your Report design should look.

Now test your report by clicking on the **Preview** button. The report is basically correct, but you may find that the Date Of Birth field is too narrow for the date to be fully displayed. We could fix this by increasing the width of the field, but a better way is to change the display properties for the field so that we no longer see all the detail of the date. To do this, right click on the field and select **Properties**. This window contains all the details of how the field is to be displayed. Change the format to **General Date** and re-test the report.

The Properties window is useful for adjusting all kinds of aspects of field display. You should explore all its capabilities when you have gained some experience with reports. The same capabilities are available for forms as well.

6.6. Sequence and Group Information in Reports

We saw how the sequence of data can be specified using the Report Wizard. We can achieve the same result when we design our own reports.

Exercise 6.3

Click on the **Sorting** and **Grouping** button on the toolbar. Access will display a window that combines these two functions in one. See Figure 6.16.

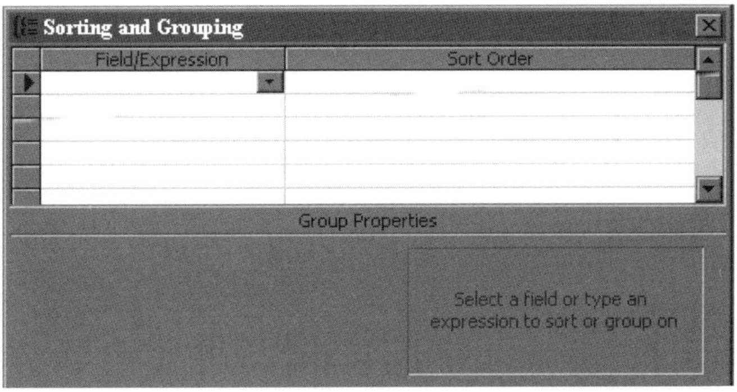

Figure 6.16 Sorting and Grouping functions combined.

In the **field/expression** column you can place the fields that you want to use to sequence the report. We want our artists in alphabetical order by name, so click on the **down arrow** and select **Name**. The **Sort Order** is already set to **Ascending** so we don't need to change this.

We could use an expression instead of a field name if we wished. See section 4.4 to revise expressions if you need this.

We could also Group together records based on the value of the field. Each group can be given a group header and footer. You can see the options for grouping in the lower part of the Sorting and Grouping window.

We don't need any grouping of data in this case so we will leave the options unchanged.

Exercise 6.4

We have been a little lazy in the way in which we have recorded the name of an artist. We have not defined any rules about how we type in names, so we have J.S. Bach and Bob Dylan. We probably should have insisted that all names be fully spelt out.

We also have another more serious problem. Our report is sorting artists based on the their name starting with the left most letters. This means that we are sorting Bob Dylan on B then on O etc. This may be what you want, but it might be better to have entered the data as Dylan, Bob so that the records will be sorted in the way you would expect. Go back to your Artist table, and change the data to reflect this.

6.7. Using Graphics in Reports

We can use graphics in reports in just the same way that we did for Forms. We can add more excitement to our design by using graphics in the Page Header and the Detail. Any graphic added to the page header will appear only in the header, but a graphic added to the detail section will be repeated for each and every record. Obviously you would not want to use large and elaborate graphics for each record, but a simple symbol can add a lot of visual appeal to a report.

Exercise 6.5

Now go back and modify the report we created at the start of this chapter with the Report Wizard. Fix the problems that we saw with the field widths and while you are doing this take note of the way that the Report Wizard has achieved its results. You should be able to replicate most of these manually using the skills that we have learned in this chapter.

Exercise 6.6

Add an appropriate graphic to the header section of the My CD Tracks report that you have been editing. Test the results to ensure that it operates as you expect.

6.8. Summary

Reports are one of the public expressions of your skill in designing a database. They will be used by people in meetings and for decision-making so it is important that they communicate information easily and clearly.

In this chapter we have explored a little of the large toolset that Access provides for constructing reports. Most of the reports you will need can be created using the Report Wizard, but we have also described the facilities you need to use in order to create a report from scratch or to edit a report produced manually or through the Report Wizard.

With the conclusion of this chapter you have now covered all the skills that you will need in order to meet the requirements of the ECDL Module 5.

Index